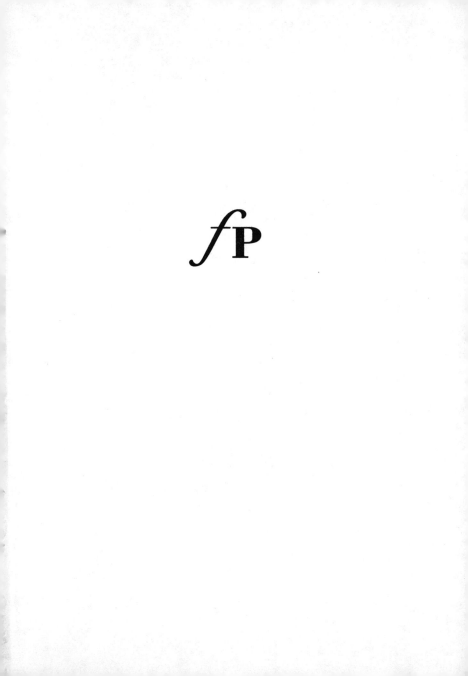

Also by Roger von Oech

A Whack on the Side of the Head

A Kick in the Seat of the Pants

Creative Whack Pack

Expect the Unexpected
(Or You Won't Find It)

A Creativity Tool Based on the
Ancient Wisdom of Heraclitus

Roger von Oech

Illustrated by George Willett

THE FREE PRESS

New York   London   Toronto   Sydney   Singapore

ƒP

THE FREE PRESS
A Division of Simon & Schuster, Inc.
1230 Avenue of the Americas
New York, NY 10020

THE FREE PRESS and colophon are trademarks
of Simon & Schuster, Inc.

Designed by Roger von Oech
Illustrations by George Willett

Manufactured in the United States of America

1   3   5   7   9   10   8   6   4   2

Library of Congress
Cataloging-in-Publication Data Is Available

ISBN 0-7432-2287-3

For information regarding special discounts for bulk purchases,
please contact Simon & Schuster Special Sales at 1-800-456-6798
or business@simonandschuster.com

To
Wendy

So deep is the creative spirit that
you will never discover its limits
even if you search every trail.

— Heraclitus

CONTENTS

Preface

HERACLITUS has long had an impact on my thinking. Indeed, trying to figure out his puzzling epigrams* led me to many of the concepts that were the basis of my first book, A *Whack on the Side of the Head.*

It was 1971 and I was studying in Germany when I was first (happily) "infected" with the Heraclitean bug of symbol, paradox, and ambiguity. I had picked up a small book entitled *Heraklit,* a Greek/German compilation of Heraclitus' writings; in it I stumbled upon this epigram: **"The way up and the way down are one and the same."** For some reason, this particular saying reached out and took hold of my mind, and I spent the next several weeks attempting to figure out its meaning. Ever since then, I've wanted to put together a creativity tool based on the ideas of this ancient Greek philosopher. That's the genesis of the work you're holding in your hands.

The title epigram, **"Expect the unexpected, or you won't find it,"** is one of my favorites for several rea-

---

*Throughout this work, I use the word "epigram" in its modern sense: a terse, witty, and often paradoxical saying. The epigram is Heraclitus' vehicle of expression.

sons. First, it is as relevant to our times as it was to those of Heraclitus. It describes a constantly changing world that amazes us with its novelty and unpredictability. It also suggests the appropriate behavior for living in such a perplexing world: be creative. If we open our minds, Heraclitus advises us, we'll discover a wondrous array of ideas to help us solve the problems that inevitably fall in our path and recognize the opportunities that occasionally flow our way. If we cultivate this attitude as we contemplate the other insights in this book, our biggest surprise will be the degree to which Heraclitus' 2,500-year-old ideas ignite our creativity!

There are at least three ways to use this book. One is to read it from start to finish as a straightforward creativity workbook. If you do this, I think you will find some worthwhile innovation strategies you can apply to your life. A second is to employ it as a daily meditation (see pages 9-13); this will allow you to dip into Heraclitus' mind for a few minutes each day to help focus your thoughts. A third possibility is to consult this work as an oracle whenever you need a jolt of ambiguity to move your thinking in a new direction (see pages 14-20). I hope you try all three!

I'd like to say a few words about my translation. The source for the ancient Greek text is T. M. Robinson's *Heraclitus* (University of Toronto Press, 1987). For most of the epigrams, I've followed standard translations, e.g., **"The sun is new each day,"** and **"Everything flows."** For a few of my renderings, however, I've been a bit more liberal. Heraclitus wrote in an oracular fashion, and in order to capture his voice, I've taken poetic license to ensure that what I believe to be the real sense of the epigram is apparent.

Let me offer an example. The most difficult insight to translate is the first one because it contains the concept *logos* (λόγος). The ancient Greek is: γινομένων γὰρ πάντων κατὰ τὸν λόγον. Literally, this epigram translates as "All things happen according to the *logos*." What is the *logos*? Its most basic meaning is "word." In the centuries before Heraclitus lived, *logos* also meant "account," "language," and "story." During Heraclitus' times, *logos* could also mean "reason," "principle," and "explanation." Six centuries later, in the Gospel according to St. John, it became *Logos* with a capital L and took on a theological meaning: "In the beginning was the Word." So what did *logos* mean to Heraclitus? Some have defined it as "logic" or "formula." I believe that what Heraclitus meant was "the organizing principle by which the cosmos orders itself." This principle manifests itself in the many different patterns we recognize. One final thought: Heraclitus, ever capable of being literal and metaphorical at the same time, knew that the "word" is "spoken." And what does the cosmos speak? I believe that "patterns" are how the *logos* is spoken to us. Thus, my translation, **"The cosmos speaks in patterns."**

I'd like to extend special thanks to my editor Rachel Klayman — her creative and disciplined guidance made a big difference. Thanks also to my friend George Willett for his illustrations. I appreciate the encouragement of Bill Shinker, Brian Selfon, Martha Levin, Suzanne Donahue, Camilla Hewitt, Stuart Kaplan, Marsh McCall, Athena von Oech, Mark Gonnerman, Alex von Oech, Tim Hurson, Franca Leeson, Michael Walker, Tim Connor, and Andrew Maisel. Finally, I wish to share my gratitude for the insights of my wife, Wendy, into this enigmatic philosopher.

Roger von Oech
July 2001
Atherton, California

Stir Your Mind
with Heraclitus

THE FIRST CREATIVITY TEACHER

Looking for inspiration? Interested in stimulating your creative juices? If so, try consulting Heraclitus, the most provocative and intriguing of the ancient Greek philosophers. His ideas about life, nature, and the cosmos were known throughout the ancient world. And even today, 2,500 years later, they retain their freshness, relevance, and — yes! — the power to stir our minds.

I've been consulting Heraclitus for many years, and he rarely lets me down. Indeed, if creative thinking involves imagining familiar things in a new light, digging below the surface to find previously undetected patterns, and finding connections among unrelated phenomena, then I believe that Heraclitus is the world's first creativity teacher. His ideas not only inspire us to think in these ways, they also provide us with strategies to understand our problems in a fresh manner. For these reasons, Heraclitus is the guide I turn to whenever I need a new perspective.

I'm not alone. So seminal are Heraclitus' ideas that over the past two and half millennia, some of the Western world's most profound thinkers have seen in them the seeds of their own beliefs. These include Plato, Aristotle, the Stoics, Marcus Aurelius, and Plotinus in antiquity; and Goethe, Hegel, Nietzsche, Carl Jung, Martin Buber, Ernst Cassirer, and T. S. Eliot in recent centuries.

Heraclitus believed that our cosmos is a wonderfully dynamic place. He also believed that most people never realize this because they live as though they are half asleep. They focus on trivial matters. They get locked into narrow ways of thinking and miss obvious solutions. As he put it, **"Many fail to grasp what's right in the palm of their hand."** His message: wake up and pay attention to what's happening within you and around you and then act on it.

Hoping to stir our minds, Heraclitus crafted his ideas as puzzling epigrams. These enigmatic sayings such as **"The most beautiful order is a heap of sweepings piled up at random,"** and **"A thing rests by changing"** have the same bracing effect on our thinking as a splash of cold water on the face.

Heraclitus' efforts to rouse the intellect and imagination have been successful. Through the ages he's earned nicknames such as "the Riddler" and "the Enigmatic One." Indeed, his use of metaphor and paradox makes him sound more like a poet or religious prophet than a philosopher. Thus, when you consult Heraclitus, you enter a vividly surreal world. His vision is filled with images of garbage-eating donkeys, avenging Furies, and pain-inflicting doctors. But against this graphic backdrop emerges a philosophy of the creative spirit. By exploring it, we can stimulate and enrich our own creativity. We'll examine Heraclitus' ideas in just a moment, but first let's take a look at his life, times, and philosophical method.

HERACLITUS' LIFE AND METHOD

According to ancient sources, Heraclitus "flourished," that is, was in his forties, around 500 B.C.E. This means that he was an almost exact contemporary of the Chinese thinkers Lao-tzu and Confucius, the Indian contemplative Siddhartha Gautama (the historical Buddha), and was only a little younger than the Persian prophet Zarathustra.

Heraclitus lived in turbulent times. During his

lifetime, long-standing empires suddenly fell while new ones arose and aggressively pressed for advantage. Most noteworthy was the rapid Persian conquest and subjugation of the Babylonian, Egyptian, Median, and Lydian empires in the sixth century B.C.E. This reversal of fortune was not lost on him. He wrote, **"War is father of all and king of all. He renders some gods, others men; he makes some slaves, others free."**

What little is known about his life is anecdotal. Heraclitus lived in the prosperous Ionian Greek coastal city-state of Ephesus in what is now western Turkey. Supposedly, he was a member of the Ephesian royal family and in line for the kingship there, but he ceded his title to his brother. It's said that he was contemptuous of other people. The second-century C.E. Greek biographer Diogenes Laertius wrote that one day a group of Ephesian citizens found Heraclitus playing dice with some children, and asked him the reason. He replied, **"Why are you surprised, you good-for-nothings? Isn't this better than playing politics with you?"**

Heraclitus was sure of his own vision, disdainful of mediocrity, and scornful of intellectual, physical, and moral laziness. This is reflected in his statement: **"If happiness consisted in the pleasures of the body, we should call oxen happy whenever they encounter fodder to eat."**

Heraclitus was present at the dawn of philosophy. He and the other early Greek philosophers — Thales, Pythagoras, Parmenides, and Democritus (later known as the "pre-Socratics" because they laid the conceptual foundations for Socrates and Plato) — were curious people who asked big questions. Philosophy means "love of wisdom" and wisdom is what they were after: What is the truth of the cosmos? How do we know? How should we live?

Heraclitus believed that reality is an enigma. As he put it, **"Things love to conceal their true nature."** But he also believed that this enigma can be understood, and that the key to solving it is finding new and different ways of thinking about it. In this quest, Heraclitus knew that it was especially important to go beyond reality's surface appearances and look at its underlying structure. In his words: **"It is wise to understand the purpose which steers all things through all things."**

To find his answers, Heraclitus devised his own means for understanding reality. He paid close attention to what was happening around him, and then thought about it until it made sense to him. He felt that consulting one's own intuition was the appropriate method for philosophical investigation. As he put it, "**I searched into myself.**" Diogenes Laertius writes, "He was no man's disciple, but said that he searched himself and learned everything from himself." Heraclitus is perhaps the first Western philosopher who starts from a point of view of stated self-awareness.

No one knows whether Heraclitus wrote a book. Perhaps he just put together a collection of his sayings. All that remains of his thought are approximately 125 epigrams, called "fragments" by the nineteenth-century German compiler of his works, Hermann Diels. All of these epigrams, interestingly enough, have been handed down to us as quotations in other ancient authors' works. It's anyone's guess whether these are exact quotations or paraphrases. Whatever the case, Heraclitus' ideas are one of the world's great treasures. How tragic to think they might have been lost for all time!

HERACLITUS' ENIGMATIC IDEAS

Heraclitus felt that the truth is precious, and that we appreciate it fully only if we have to actively participate in finding it. His style — similar to a Zen teacher's paradoxical *koan* or a Delphic Oracle's ambiguous prophecy — is designed to "whack" us out of our habitual thought patterns so that we can look at what we're doing in a fresh way.

Making sense of his enigmatic ideas is a big challenge! Reading them can make us shake our heads and ask, "What does he mean by that?" Indeed, I can picture one of his students complaining to him, "You give us your ideas but don't reveal their meaning." To which I can imagine Heraclitus' reply: "How would you like it if someone offered you a juicy apple and chewed it up before giving it to you? No one can find your meaning for you but you."

It's best to think of each epigram as a creativity exercise that has to be solved in order to unlock its meaning. To solve each exercise, we need to be imaginative, tolerate ambiguity, reverse our expectations, view things metaphorically, and probe for hidden meanings. In short, we need to adopt the mindset we might use when we're creating something.

I've selected thirty epigrams which I believe best express Heraclitus' philosophy of the creative spirit. I call these his Creative Insights. They are listed on pages 12 and 13. Viewed as a whole, these thirty jewels of thought provide us with a set of tools on how to be more creative. Take time to get to know them. How do they strike you? Which ones make immediate sense? Which are puzzling? Which ones contradict others?

There's no need to rush! These Insights have been around for 2,500 years and they aren't going anywhere. Indeed, you may wish to meditate on just one Insight a day, perhaps focusing on Creative Insight #1 on the first day of the month, #2 on the second, and so on to #30 on the thirtieth. The meditation can be as simple as a few moments dwelling on the significance of the idea and its application to your life. Or you may wish to use the Insight as a lens through which to view your experience during the day. It's fascinating to see how each Insight comes alive when you do this.

For example, I can remember one time when I was stumped by a design problem and **"That which opposes produces a benefit"** was my Insight for the day. I thought about the message and realized that I needed to discard my objective and seek out a different one. I was delighted with the result. On another occasion, I was at loggerheads with an old friend and opened to, **"When there is no sun, we can see the evening stars."** I decided to spend the day listening and attempting to keep my ego in check. As a result, I discovered some qualities in my friend that I had been overlooking. Still another time, the Insight *du jour* was **"Dogs bark at what they don't understand."** That day I made a special effort to see the value of the weird ideas that came my way.

If you wish to develop a creative outlook, I heartily recommend working through the Creative Insights on a regular basis. When you're done with each cycle, start anew. Not only will they provoke different and original thoughts each month, they will also become wise companions whose guidance you will welcome!

THE CREATIVE INSIGHTS OF HERACLITUS

1. The cosmos speaks in patterns.

2. Expect the unexpected, or you won't find it.

3. Everything flows.

4. You can't step into the same river twice.

5. That which opposes produces a benefit.

6. A wonderful harmony is created when we join together the seemingly unconnected.

7. If all things turned to smoke, the nose would become the discerning organ.

8. The Sun will not exceed its limits, because the avenging Furies, ministers of Justice, would find out.

9. Lovers of wisdom must open their minds to very many things.

10. I searched into myself.

11. Knowing many things doesn't teach insight.

12. Many fail to grasp what's right in the palm of their hand.

13. When there is no sun, we can see the evening stars.

14. The most beautiful order is a heap of sweepings piled up at random.

15. Things love to conceal their true nature.

16 Those who approach life like a child playing a game, moving and pushing pieces, possess the power of kings.

17 Sea water is both pure and polluted: for fish it is drinkable and life-giving; for humans undrinkable and destructive.

18 On a circle, an end point can also be a beginning point.

19 It is disease that makes health pleasant, hunger that makes fullness good, and weariness that makes rest sweet.

20 The doctor inflicts pain to cure suffering.

21 The way up and the way down are one and the same.

22 A thing rests by changing.

23 The barley-wine drink falls apart unless it is stirred.

24 While we're awake, we share one universe, but in sleep we each turn away to a world of our own.

25 Dogs bark at what they don't understand.

26 Donkeys prefer garbage to gold.

27 Every walking animal is driven to its purpose with a whack.

28 There is a greater need to extinguish arrogance than a blazing fire.

29 Your character is your destiny.

30 The sun is new each day.

Use Heraclitus as an Oracle

Let's suppose that you're currently dealing with a challenging issue. It could be a perplexing problem that resists your best efforts. Or, maybe it's a difficult decision you need to make. Perhaps this issue is even keeping you up at night. You've tried various approaches to resolve it but you keep coming up empty. You know you've got some good ideas inside you, but you're baffled on how to get to them. You think to yourself, "What can I do to find inspiration?" Here's an answer: consult Heraclitus as an oracle.

This makes good sense because the tool implicit in Heraclitus' thought (and perhaps explicit in his long lost works) is the oracle. Indeed, the model for his writings appears to be the Delphic Oracle. Heraclitus acknowledges this influence when he says, **"The Lord whose oracle is at Delphi neither indicates clearly nor conceals but gives a sign."** In his writings, Heraclitus does pretty much the same thing.

Before we consult Heraclitus as an oracle, let's take a moment to understand what an oracle is and does. Over the millennia, many cultures have developed their own versions of this intuitive tool. Some examples include: the ancient Chinese *I Ching,* the Egyptian Tarot, the Nordic Runes, and the North American Indian Medicine Wheel. Most oracles consist of a series of messages from which the questioner randomly selects. The purpose of querying an oracle is not so much to foretell the future as to enable the questioner to delve more deeply into his own intuition when dealing with a problem.

Probably the most famous oracle in the ancient world was the one at Delphi in mainland Greece. And one of that oracle's best known prophecies was made in the year 480 B.C.E., when Greece and Persia were at war. Under Xerxes, the Persians had invaded the Greek mainland and conquered two-thirds of the country. Naturally, the Athenian leaders were concerned as to which course of action they should take against the oncoming Persians. They realized, however, that before any decision could be made they should send some suppliants to Delphi to get a reading from the oracle. The suppliants made the journey and received the following prophecy: "The wooden wall will save you and your children."

The suppliants took these words back to Athens.

At first the leaders weren't sure what the prophecy meant. Then it was suggested that they should build a wooden wall on the Acropolis and take a defensive stand behind it. That's what the "wooden wall" meant — a barricade on the Acropolis.

But the leaders knew that the oracle was intentionally ambiguous in order to force them to go beyond the first right answer. So they tried to think of various contexts — literal and metaphorical — in which the words "the wooden wall will save you and your children" made sense. After some thought, they came up with another idea. Could the "wooden wall" refer to their scores of wooden-hulled ships? From a distance, lined up next to one another, the ships would indeed look like a "wooden wall." The leaders decided that the battle should be a naval one rather than a land one. It was an auspicious decision, for the Athenians routed the Persians in the famous naval battle of Salamis. Moral: The oracle's ambiguity had forced the leaders to consult the wisdom of their own intuition, and consider alternatives.

I believe that we can use this same oracular approach when consulting Heraclitus. Let's go through the three basic steps one by one.

FIRST: You need to have a specific question on which you would like a fresh perspective. Clear your mind so that you are in a receptive state. Now formulate your question. One question I like to ask is:

"What do I need to focus on to gain understanding in my current situation?"

SECOND: You need an "answer" that addresses your question. This book contains thirty such answers. Which one is best for you? Why not use the Creative Insight that corresponds to today's date? For example, you'd turn to #12 on the twelfth of the month, or #4 on the fourth. Better still, why not select an Insight at random? Open this book anywhere; the Insight you've picked is your answer. Another method for selecting a random Insight is to put your finger or pen down on a number on page 18. This number corresponds to the Insight that's the answer to your question. (Also, many game stores carry a thirty-sided die called a "tricosahedron." Try rolling one of these to select your random number.)

Why random Insights? Since we tend to use the same problem-solving approaches repeatedly, we

21	25	29	02	06	10	14	18	22	26	10	15	20	25	30	01	06	11	16	21	26	02	07	12	17	22	27
08	13	18	23	28	04	09	09	11	13	15	17	19	21	23	25	27	01	02	03	04	05	12	17	22	27	03
13	18	23	28	04	09	14	19	24	29	01	02	03	04	05	06	07	08	09	10	11	12	23	25	27	29	30
06	07	08	09	10	11	12	13	30	03	07	11	15	19	23	27	05	14	15	16	17	18	19	20	21	22	23
25	26	27	28	29	30	02	04	06	08	10	12	14	16	18	20	22	24	26	28	30	01	03	05	07	09	11
15	17	19	21	23	25	27	29	30	28	26	24	22	20	18	16	14	12	10	08	06	04	02	29	27	25	23
19	17	15	13	11	09	07	05	03	01	03	06	09	12	15	18	21	24	27	30	01	04	07	10	13	16	19
25	28	02	05	08	11	14	17	20	23	26	29	04	08	12	16	20	24	28	01	05	09	13	17	21	25	29
06	10	14	18	22	26	30	03	07	11	15	19	23	27	05	10	15	20	25	30	01	06	11	21	26	02	07
17	22	27	03	08	13	18	23	28	04	09	09	11	13	15	17	19	21	23	25	27	29	30	28	26	24	22
18	16	14	12	10	08	06	04	02	29	27	25	23	21	19	17	15	13	11	09	07	05	03	01	03	06	09
15	18	21	24	27	30	01	04	29	01	02	03	04	05	06	07	08	09	10	11	12	13	14	15	13	14	15
17	18	19	20	21	22	23	24	25	26	27	28	29	30	02	04	06	08	10	12	14	16	18	20	22	24	26
30	01	03	05	07	09	11	15	17	19	21	16	17	18	19	20	21	07	10	13	16	19	22	25	28	02	05
11	14	17	20	23	26	29	04	08	12	16	20	24	28	01	05	09	13	17	21	25	29	02	06	10	14	18
26	30	03	07	11	15	19	23	27	05	10	15	20	25	30	01	06	11	16	21	26	02	07	26	24	22	07
16	14	12	10	08	06	04	02	29	27	25	23	21	19	17	15	13	11	09	07	05	03	01	03	06	09	12
18	21	24	27	30	01	04	07	10	13	16	19	22	25	28	02	05	08	11	16	19	22	26	30	03	07	11
08	12	16	20	24	28	01	05	09	13	17	21	25	29	02	06	10	14	18	22	26	30	03	07	11	15	19
27	05	10	15	20	25	30	01	06	11	16	21	26	02	07	12	17	22	27	03	08	13	18	23	28	04	09
19	24	22	23	24	25	26	27	28	29	30	02	04	06	08	10	12	14	16	18	20	22	24	26	28	30	01
05	07	09	11	13	15	17	19	23	25	27	29	30	28	26	24	22	20	18	16	14	12	10	08	06	04	02
27	25	23	21	19	17	15	13	11	09	07	05	03	01	03	06	09	12	15	18	21	24	27	30	01	04	07
13	16	19	22	25	28	02	05	08	11	14	17	20	23	26	29	04	08	12	16	20	24	28	01	05	09	13
10	25	29	02	06	10	14	18	22	26	30	03	07	11	15	19	23	27	05	10	15	20	25	30	01	06	11
21	26	02	07	12	17	22	27	03	08	13	18	23	28	04	09	14	19	24	29	01	02	03	04	05	06	07
09	10	11	12	13	14	15	16	17	18	19	20	21	22	23	24	25	26	27	28	29	30	02	04	06	08	10
14	16	18	20	22	24	26	28	30	01	03	05	07	09	11	13	15	17	19	21	23	25	27	29	30	28	26
22	20	18	16	14	12	10	08	06	04	02	29	27	25	23	21	19	17	15	13	11	09	07	05	03	01	03
09	12	15	18	21	24	27	30	01	04	07	10	13	16	19	22	25	28	02	05	08	11	14	17	20	23	26
04	08	12	16	20	24	28	01	05	09	13	17	21	25	29	02	06	10	14	18	22	26	30	03	07	11	15
23	27	05	10	15	20	25	30	01	06	11	16	21	26	02	07	12	17	22	27	03	08	13	18	23	28	04
08	13	18	23	28	04	09	14	19	24	22	23	24	25	26	27	28	29	30	02	04	06	08	10	12	14	16
20	22	24	26	28	30	01	03	05	07	09	11	13	15	17	19	21	23	28	02	05	08	11	14	17	20	23
29	04	08	12	16	20	24	28	01	05	09	13	17	21	25	29	02	06	10	14	18	22	26	30	03	07	11
19	23	27	05	10	15	20	25	30	01	06	11	16	21	26	02	07	12	17	22	27	03	08	13	18	23	28
09	14	19	24	29	01	02	03	04	05	06	07	08	09	10	11	12	13	14	15	16	17	18	19	20	21	22
24	25	27	28	29	30	02	04	06	08	10	12	14	16	18	20	22	24	26	28	30	01	03	05	07	09	16
21	23	25	27	29	30	21	25	29	02	06	10	14	18	22	26	10	15	20	25	30	01	06	11	16	21	26
07	12	17	22	27	03	08	13	18	23	28	04	09	09	11	13	15	17	19	21	23	25	27	01	02	03	04
12	17	22	27	03	08	13	18	23	28	04	09	14	19	24	29	01	02	03	04	05	06	07	08	09	10	11

usually come up with the same answers. Random Insights can force us to look at our problems in a way we would not have otherwise, and this does wonders to stir our thinking. I think Heraclitus would like this approach. After all, he did say: **"The most beautiful order is a heap of sweepings piled up at random."**

THIRD: How does the Creative Insight relate to your question? What story does it tell? What sense can you make out of it? Try to think of as many contexts as possible in which the Insight makes sense. Be literal in your interpretation. Be meta-phorical. Be off-the-wall. Be serious. Don't worry how practical or logical you are. What's important is to give free rein to your thinking.

Most Insights will trigger an immediate response. Sometimes, however, you'll look at one and think, "This has nothing to do with my question," and be tempted to dismiss it. Don't. Force yourself to make a connection. Often those ideas that initially seem the least relevant turn out to be the most important because they point to something that you've been completely overlooking. For example, if **"Donkeys**

prefer garbage to gold" or **"The doctor inflicts pain to cure suffering"** aren't the usual things you think of when dealing with a problem, then your reflections on these Insights are likely to give you new perspective on your question.

PUT ON YOUR CREATIVITY HAT

The rest of this book contains my interpretations of the Creative Insights. Many of the Insights have multiple interpretations; most of these complement one another, but a few are contradictory. If you disagree with or dislike these interpretations, so much the better! I encourage you to put on your "creativity hat" and come up with your own ideas. That's the beauty of working with Heraclitus — there's no one right answer! Indeed, sometimes I don't even agree with myself. If, as Heraclitus put it, **"You can't step into the same river twice,"** then my own state of mind can never be quite the same, and my own interpretations change. And the same will be true for you: the Creative Insights will continue to take on new and fresh meanings.

The
Creative Insights
of Heraclitus

"The cosmos speaks in patterns."

γινομένων γὰρ πάντων κατὰ τὸν λόγον.

FIND A PATTERN. If the cosmos reveals its secrets to us in patterns, then we need to listen for them. Indeed, we should use all of our senses. Fortunately, much of what we call "human intelligence" is our ability to recognize and discover new patterns. This is an important power; based on these patterns, we form our expectations of what we think we'll experience as we go about the business of living.

For those of you who like pattern recognition puzzles, here are two. First: the letters of the alphabet can be grouped into four different categories: (1) A, M; (2) B, C, D, E, K; (3) F, G, J, K, L; and (4) H, I. Figure out the pattern, and place the remaining thirteen letters in their appropriate categories. Second: find what the following words have in common: laughing, starburst, calmness, crabcake, stuffed, canopy, hijack.

We find patterns all around us. We see similarities: stellar galaxies and water emptying out of a bathtub both spiral in the same way. We calculate probabilities: the more graffiti on the back of a road sign, the more difficult it will be to hitchhike a ride from that spot. We observe tendencies: terminally ill nursing-home patients are more likely to die after a holiday than before. We recognize self-fulfilling prophecies: people who are interested in synchronicity find meaningful coincidences almost everywhere. We see relationships: the tighter a government's restrictions on its press, the less prosperous that society is likely to be.

We figure out sequences: Fibonacci numbers consist of adding together the two previous numbers to create the current one: 1, 1, 2, 3, 5, 8, 13, 21, 34, 55, 89, 144 . . . .* We arrive at correlations: on the whole, bigger animals such as whales, elephants, and humans live longer than smaller animals such as mice, hummingbirds, and snakes. We

---

*"Fibonacci numbers" are named after the nickname of their discoverer, the fourteenth-century Italian mathematician Leonardo Pisano. They describe such things as the running total of successive generations of rabbits, and also the number of growing points in branching plants. Interestingly, the ratio of the current number to the previous one approximates 1.618 — known to the Greeks as the "golden mean." This number defines the proportions of numerous manmade objects — from the Parthenon to a common playing card. The golden mean also occurs throughout nature in such things as sunflower patterns, nautilus spirals, and ocean waves.

discern behaviors: people in crowded elevators tend to look at the ceiling. And we discover personal inclinations: when I'm hungry or tired I'm more likely to get irritated.

How do we find patterns? Often they just pop into my head. But I also find them by getting into a "pattern-seeking" frame of mind. First I notice something that has occurred more than once. Then I focus my thinking and look for or remember other things related to it. Yes, it's a wonderful arrangement the human mind and the cosmos have: once we start looking for patterns, the cosmos accommodates us by letting us find them!

Indeed, have you ever noticed that when you learn a new word — say "zygote" or "equanimity" — you proceed to hear or think of uses for that word a half dozen times in the next few days? Similarly, when you're looking for a new car and you narrow the choice down to a single make and model, you're likely to see that type of car at every traffic light.

❖ **What patterns do you see in your current situation? What patterns do you expect to see? How are these expectations guiding your thinking?**

FIND A REASON. Let's go one step further. Life can be seen simply as a series of events that just happen. But if we heed Heraclitus' advice and look for patterns, we may discover a larger logic at work. Remember the old adage, "Once is an instance, twice may be a coincidence, but three or more times make a pattern." ❖ **What story do you think the cosmos is telling you? Have you noticed any "coincidences" in your daily life that suggest the existence of a larger pattern?**

CHANGE YOUR VIEWPOINT. To discover new patterns, often it's necessary to change our point of view. An illustration of this is a story told by psychiatrist Paul Watzlawick about a strange phenomenon that took place in Seattle in the late 1950s. It seems that people began discovering small pockmarks on their car windshields. As more and more of these tiny indentations were found, the public became alarmed. Two theories arose to explain the pitting. Some said that atomic tests by the Russians had contaminated the atmosphere and this, combined with Seattle's moist climate, had produced fallout that was returning to earth in a glass-etching dew. Others speculated that tiny residual acid drops from Seattle's recently constructed roads were being flung against the windshields. As Seattle drivers worked themselves into a frenzy, the federal government sent a team of experts to investigate the mystery. Their finding: the windshield pitting was an old phenomenon, not a new one. All windshields develop "scars" as a car ages; it's part of the normal wear and tear on a vehicle.

This is a good example of a kind of mass hysteria. How did it develop? As the reports of the windshield pits came to the attention of more and more people, they checked their own cars, usually by looking through the glass from the *outside* of the car. From this vantage point it's easy to see the pitting, which is usually invisible from the inside. What had broken out in Seattle was an epidemic not of windshield pitting, but of reverse windshield viewing. By changing their point of view, people discovered something that had always been there but they had never noticed. ❖ **What patterns might you discover if you change your point of view?**

FIND A PATTERN IN MANY PLACES. One method I use to open my mind is to look at a single pattern in many different contexts. For example, let's take a look at the magnificent number 12. It's quite useful for dividing: twelve of anything can be evenly split into halves, thirds, quarters, and sixths. But even more important, I believe that "twelve" is deeply embedded in the human psyche. Early humans must have been quite impressed with the relationship between the two brightest heavenly bodies, the sun and the moon. From the moment when the sun reaches its highest point on the meridian (noon on the summer solstice) until it does so again one year later, the moon waxes and wanes a total of twelve times. Twelve times! If, as Heraclitus put it, "The cosmos speaks in patterns," then this very fundamental pattern must have had cosmic significance to early humans grasping for meaning.

"Twelve" is a pattern that manifests itself in life, nature, religion, mathematics, technology, design, and culture in many interesting and provocative ways. There are twelve months in a year, twelve hours on the face of a clock, and twelve signs of the zodiac. Achilles gave King Priam twelve days to prepare for his son Hector's funeral in the *Iliad*. Twelve is the number of axes through which Odysseus had to shoot an arrow to win Penelope. A regular dodecahedron has twelve pentagonal sides. A musical octave has twelve chromatic tones. There were twelve tribes of Israel, twelve disciples of Jesus, and twelve men who have walked on the moon. The Twelver Shi'a Muslim sect believes that the Twelfth *Imam* (Islamic preceptor) did not die. There are twelve days of Christmas, twelve steps in recovery programs, twelve jurors on American juries, and twelve buttons on touch-tone telephones. A perfect game in bowling consists of twelve consecutive strikes. And finally, one more than twelve feels "unlucky." ❖ **Think of a pattern or concept. How does this pattern find expression in different arenas of life? Do any of these manifestations provide an insight into your own situation?**

"Expect the unexpected, or you won't find it."

ἐὰν μὴ ἔλπηται ἀνέλπιστον, οὐκ ἐξευρήσει.

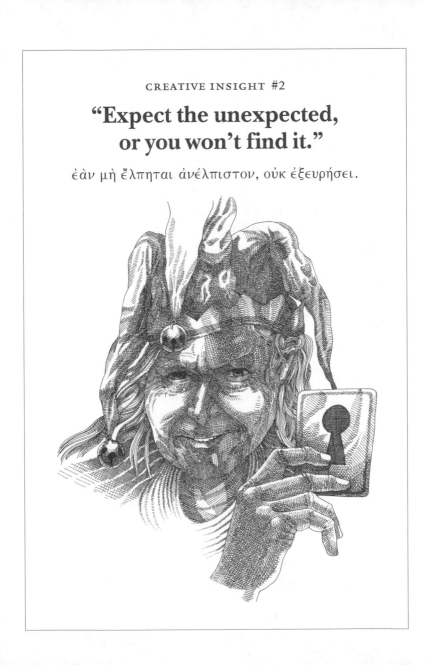

DROP AN ASSUMPTION. Folklore has it that ex-plorer Christopher Columbus challenged some Spanish courtiers to stand an egg on end. They tried but were unable to keep it from rolling over. Columbus then hard-boiled the egg and squashed one end of it to create a base. Not fair, the court-iers protested. "Don't be silly," Columbus replied. "You just assumed more than you needed to."

Assumptions are one of the mind's great suc-cess stories. They allow us to anticipate what will happen in a variety of situations and prepare ap-propriately. If, for example, your boss has been grouchy the last nine Monday mornings, then you'll probably assume that this coming Monday morning isn't the ideal time to ask for a raise. The trouble with assumptions is that the past isn't al-ways a reliable predictor of the future. The more assumptions we make, the more likely we are to see only what we expect to see, and the less likely we are to find the unexpected. (Maybe your boss won the lottery over the weekend. Or fell in love!)

A seminar exercise I like to do involves making paper airplanes. Here's how it works: I assign the participants to different teams and give each team fifty sheets of paper. Then I draw a line at the back of the room. Each team has five minutes to see how many airplanes it can make that can fly past the line, and the one with the most is the winner. The most common approach is to fold the sheets into conventional paper airplane shapes. But the winning design, more often than not, is a sheet of paper that has been crumpled into a ball. The crumpled balls of paper invariably "fly" past the line — the only criterion that has to be satisfied in the exercise. And the losing teams immediately grasp that what most hobbled their thinking was their assumptions about what a paper airplane is supposed to look like.

Inventor Thomas Edison had a simple test he used to measure the "unexpectedness quotient" of prospective employees. He would invite a candidate to lunch and serve a bowl of soup. He would then watch to see whether the person salted his soup before tasting it. If he did, he wouldn't be offered the job. Edison felt that people are more open to different possibilities if they don't salt their experience of life before tasting it. ❖ **What assumptions can you drop in your current situation? In what ways are you "salting your experience" before tasting it?**

BE WILLING TO BE LED ASTRAY. When we go off the beaten path, we often find something better or more exciting than what we were originally looking for. For example, physicist Karl Jansky improvised a new antenna to study the effects of telephone static. Instead, he discovered radio waves from the Milky Way galaxy, and in the process helped create the science of radioastronomy. In 1856, chemist William Perkin searched for a synthetic quinine to combat malaria. Instead, he discovered a dyestuff (he called it "Mauveline," which the public shortened to mauve) that was the first practical synthetic color. In 1984, biologist Alec Jeffreys studied the gene for the muscle protein myoglobin hoping to gain an understanding of how genes evolve. Instead, he stumbled upon a stretch of DNA in the middle of the gene that varied greatly from one individual to another. This led to his pioneering work in the creation of "DNA fingerprinting," which has revolutionized not only forensic science but also other fields such as anthropology and epidemiology.

Think of the times in your own life when one thing has led to something entirely different. How did you get interested in your line of work? How about the times you've gone to the library in search of a particular book, and then found something even better on the shelf behind you? As writer Franklin Adams put it, "I find that a great part of the information I have was acquired by looking up something and finding something else on the way."

How can we prepare ourselves for the unexpected? I suggest that we: (1) loosen our preconceptions about what we expect to find in any given situation; (2) pay special attention to the anomalous rather than ignoring it; and, (3) use what we discover as stepping stones to something very different. Why don't we adopt this outlook more often? A major reason is that in order to get things done, we tend to filter out information that strikes us as "irrelevant." Indeed, I find that I'm less likely to find the unexpected when I'm in a hurry or narrowly focused on a specific task. Conversely, when I'm relaxed or playful, there's a greater probability that unexpected things will flow my way.
❖ **In what new directions can your situation lead you? What might open up if you abandoned your original objective?**

PREPARE FOR UNINTENDED CONSEQUENCES. Pursuing our dreams or trying to solve our problems in unusual ways can bring great rewards, but it can also lead to trouble. In fact, sometimes it can bring rewards and troubles at the same time! Remember the story of the ancient Phrygian king Midas? According to legend, Midas so loved gold that when the god Dionysus offered to grant him his deepest wish, he asked that all he touched be turned to this precious metal. At first, Midas was delighted with his wealth-creating power, but after discovering that his contact made food inedible and his embraces rendered loved ones lifeless, he soon realized that getting what you want can have unintended — and undesirable — consequences.

Sometimes the solution to a problem can even make the problem worse that it originally was. In the 1960s, engineers in what is now Bangladesh designed huge off-shore structures to protect coastal areas from the erosion caused by high tides and natural catastrophes. Unfortunately, the structures also encouraged a false sense of security, which led to massive "squatting" on nearby land. When a cyclone struck in 1970, it took the lives of nearly half a million people, in no small part because so many lived in unsafe coastal areas. Thus, the government's efforts to protect residents had unintended consequences — they indirectly caused more deaths.

During the Soviet-Afghan war, the Soviets unleashed brutal attacks on the civilian population, believing that this would intimidate the Afghans into submission. Ironically, the attacks had an unexpected and opposite result. Because Afghan warriors traditionally stayed close to home to guard their families, the Soviets' driving Afghan women and children into refugee camps liberated the Mujahideen from family responsibilities and turned them into a more formidable opponent.

Finally, the coach of a leading crew team invited a meditation instructor to teach awareness methods to his crew. He hoped that such training would enhance their rowing effectiveness. As they learned more about meditation, they became more synchronized and their strokes became smoother. The irony is that they went slower. It turned out that they became more interested in being in harmony than in winning. ❖ **What might be the unintended consequences of implementing your idea?**

PAY ATTENTION TO SMALL THINGS. In 1960, meteorologist Edward Lorenz was attempting to model weather patterns through computer simulation. He plugged data on wind speed, air pressure, and temperature into three equations that were linked, such that the calculations from the first were fed into the second which then fed its results into the third and so on back to the first, thus creating a mathematical feedback loop. With this simple model, Lorenz was able to predict the weather with some accuracy.

One day, Lorenz needed to recheck the results of a long calculation. He decided to take a shortcut, and entered the same data he had used previously but rounded it to the nearest one thousandth rather than to the nearest one millionth (for example, .506 instead of .506127). He thought this would have little impact on the overall result — perhaps no more than one tenth of one percent. When he looked at his printout patterns, however, he was amazed to discover that they were significantly different from the first run. He soon realized that even an infinitesimal change in the numbers reflecting wind, temperature, or pressure conditions would be magnified by the feedback process, and the end result would be greatly altered. This discovery ultimately led Lorenz to wonder: "Does the flap of a butterfly's wing in Brazil cause a tornado in Texas?"

Since then, the Butterfly Effect has become a rich metaphor used in many fields outside physics to describe how a very small change in a variable in a dynamic system can have a huge impact on how that system behaves. Indeed, there are countless "butterflies" of subtle varieties and colors exerting their power throughout our everyday life. One well-known example is that of the O-rings on the space shuttle *Challenger*. In 1986, the slightly defective rings combined with cold weather caused the explosion of its fuel tanks soon after launch. Other examples: a stock rumor that quickly moves through the trading floor causing the market to crash; a runner who goes out just a little too fast in the early stages of a marathon and prematurely builds up excess lactic acid in his system, causing him to "hit the wall" three-fourths of the way into the race; and a slow vehicle in the fast lane of the freeway during rush hour that disrupts traffic flow for miles.

The Butterfly Effect should make us more conscious of the consequences of our actions. If the snap of our fingers or a pinecone falling from its tree can change the weather halfway around the world, imagine the impact you can have with a single rude remark. Conversely, think about what a word of encouragement or a pat on the back can do for someone working on a difficult problem.

As science writer Philip Goldberg puts it, "Like the Hindu concept of *karma,* the Butterfly Effect suggests that cause and effect are applicable in the universe even if the pattern is indecipherable and the precise causes of our predicaments, rooted far away in time and space, are ultimately unfathomable." Computer scientist Douglas Hofstadter — in a remark reminiscent of Heraclitus — puts it in a slightly different way: "It turns out than an eerie type of chaos can lurk just behind a facade of order — yet, deep inside the chaos lurks an eerier type of order." Perhaps this is one of the deeper truths behind "expecting the unexpected." ❖ **What small changes in your situation might have very large unexpected consequences? What "butterflies" are at work?**

"Everything flows."

πάντα ῥεῖ.

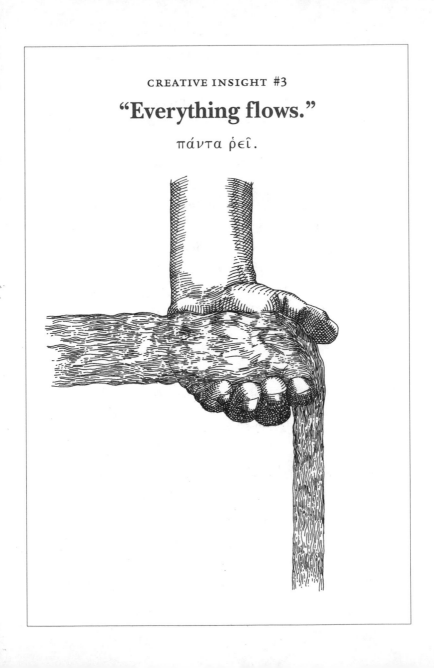

WITNESS CHANGE. This is Heraclitus' most famous epigram. All things — even those we think are stable — continually change over time, he tells us. Often the change is predictable, as in the flow of seasons from spring to summer to autumn or the stages of a butterfly from egg to caterpillar to chrysalis to adult. Sometimes, however, the change appears random and inexplicable, such as a rapid increase in solar flare activity or a sudden outbreak of a deadly virus. Yet, if we're discerning, we can find patterns within this change.

For example, most recent technology revolutions — from the telephone and the automobile to computers and the Internet — have moved through similar periods of development: free-wheeling experimentation, massive capitalization, hyper-competition, shakeout and consolidation. Another familiar change pattern, first identified by psychiatrist Elisabeth Kübler-Ross, is that of the phases of grief through which the dying pass: denial, anger, bargaining, depression, and acceptance.

The process of change can take many forms: your relationship with your parents will run one course; your role with your children will run a different one. Your attitude about work will run still another. In addition, we might extend Heraclitus' water metaphor by noting that things "flow" at different rates: a glacier flows at one speed, a flooding stream at another, a lazy river at another, a waterfall at another, and a stagnant pond at still another (it evaporates).* Indeed, if we don't notice the change, perhaps we're not looking at things in quite the right way. If you observe a block of iron over a two-minute period, you wouldn't say that it's flowing; but if you look at it over several years, you see rust and corrosion. Conversely, some things change so quickly that unless we alter our perspective, it's difficult to understand how different things are related to one another in the same process.

---

*An interesting way to track your own "flow" is to gather a series of photographs of yourself over the past twenty or more years. Notice the ways in which you've changed. Are there times when there is a sparkle in your eyes? How about changes in weight, hair, and facial features? Can you see the impact of significant events in your appearance? This exercise can also be done with famous people, notably American presidents. It's striking how forcibly the currents of time flow through them. My personal favorites are the rapid changes in two wartime presidents: Abraham Lincoln and Franklin Roosevelt.

One person who has had a long interest in the underlying patterns in which things "flow" is fractal geometrician Benoit Mandelbrot. Mandelbrot studied the historical data of some of the world's great rivers, in particular the Nile. He characterized the patterns he saw by borrowing from stories from Genesis: the "Joseph Effect" and the "Noah Effect."

The "Joseph Effect" — after Joseph's interpretation of Pharaoh's dream of seven fat cows and seven gaunt ones to mean that there would be seven prosperous years followed by seven lean ones — describes *persistence*. He discovered that trends tend to persist; that is, if a place has been suffering drought it's likely it will suffer more of the same. In other words, things tend to be the way they have been recently. Some examples: healthy people tend to stay healthy; winning teams tend to keep on winning; and products that have been successful for the past five years will probably be successful this month.

On the other hand, the "Noah Effect" — after the story of the great flood — describes *discontinuity*. Mandelbrot found that when something changes, it can change abruptly. For example, a stock priced at $40 a share can quickly fall to $5 without ever being priced at $30 or $20 if something significant triggers its collapse. As science writer James Gleick stated, "The Noah and Joseph Effects push in different directions, but they add up to this: trends in nature are real, but they can vanish as quickly as they come." Thus, we can expect what's been happening to continue to happen, but we should also expect the unexpected. ❖ **What patterns describe the "flow" of your situation? What long-term trends are at work? Have you noticed any abrupt changes?**

APPRECIATE TURBULENCE. In addition to discovering that "everything flows," Heraclitus surely also observed that most of this flow is turbulent. As designer Peter Stevens put it, "Turbulence forms the primordial pattern, the chaos that was *in the beginning*." For example, open a faucet part way and the water that streams out will be smooth, uniform, and glassy; this is known as "laminar" flow. Open the faucet a little more, however, and the water becomes roiled and chaotic; this is "turbulent" flow. Similarly, when smoke rises straight up from a stick of burning incense it is even and smooth; when it rises a bit higher, it becomes filled with zigzagging eddies. Indeed, eddies are a distinguishing feature of turbulence. We see them when we pour cream into coffee and white marbled swirls appear or, on a larger scale, in satellite pictures of advancing weather fronts. On a cosmic scale, we're awestruck by their presence within exploding nebulae and spiraling galaxies.

Turbulence is one of the great mysteries of our existence.* This much, though, we can say: it is the result of materials of different densities, viscosities, and speeds acting on one another. Although we expect to find eddies in turbulent flow, we cannot predict when any specific eddy will come into being or die away, or how it will interact with others. Thus, unpredictability is the hallmark of turbulent situations. The negative side of turbulence, of course, is that it can be destructive; for example, it can capsize ships and rupture pipes. Its great benefit, however, is the dynamic churning and mixing of materials that are separated or stratified when at rest. For example,

---

*It's said that when German physicist Werner Heisenberg — "Mr. Uncertainty Principle" himself — was on his deathbed, he said, "When I get to heaven, I'll have two questions for God: 'Why relativity? Why turbulence?' I think He may have some answers to the first one."

turbulence in our atmosphere causes water vapor and carbon dioxide to be more evenly distributed over a wider area; turbulent currents in the ocean spread nutrients to a more diverse array of ecological niches; and, within animals, turbulence aids the exchange of gases in blood circulation.

As a metaphor for the creative process, we can say that turbulent forces within an individual, relationship, or group can stir together ideas, thoughts, and opinions that might not otherwise be joined. These forces can also help dislodge limiting assumptions, and compel people to jettison beliefs that are no longer appropriate. As historian Chester Starr put it, "Every so often civilization seems to work itself into a corner from which further progress is virtually impossible along the lines then apparent; if new ideas are to have a chance the old systems must be so throughly shaken that they lose their dominance." For example, Genghis Khan's Mongol invasion of China in the thirteenth century shook up what had become a stagnant country. The ensuing mixture of Mongol military tactics and expert horsemanship with Chinese iron technology and administrative knowhow led to political unity, a flourishing commercial sector, and expanded trade routes.

At its best, turbulence can be invigorating and stimulating.* On the downside, it can leave us feeling confused, battered, and enervated. At its worst, turbulence can lead to debilitating chaos. For example, Chinese leader Mao Zedong generated massive turbulence within his own country in 1966 with his "Cultural Revolution." By unleashing a brutal force — the Red Guards — on his own people and institutions, Mao hoped to create a vibrant society by blasting apart old habits, thinking, and customs. But since he provided few practical rules apart from his ideological *Little Red Book* on how to achieve this goal, his destructive actions led to an economic and social mess from which China took many years to recover.

❖ **How would some turbulence energize the flow of your present situation? How could it be corrosive?**

---

*Think of the famous Harry Lime speech (written and performed by Orson Welles) in the 1949 film, *The Third Man*: "In Italy for thirty years under the Borgias they had warfare, terror, murder and bloodshed, but they produced Michelangelo, Leonardo da Vinci, and the Renaissance. In Switzerland they had brotherly love and five hundred years of democracy and peace, and what did that produce? The cuckoo clock."

"You can't step into the same river twice."

ποταμῷ γὰρ οὐκ ἔστιν
ἐμβῆναι δὶς τῷ αὐτῷ.

RETHINK YOUR APPROACH. A flowing river constantly changes its contents: the waters in front of us move on and others replenish them. Heraclitus says the cosmos functions in the same way: new things come into being, others die, and everything is transformed. We have only to look at what's happening around us to see that this is true. New laws are enacted and others are no longer enforced. New social and political movements gain momentum while others become spent and irrelevant. New styles of behavior and expression become fashionable and others are relegated to the dust-heap. Thus, we need to continually review our assumptions and make sure that the strategies we employ are appropriate to the problems and opportunities before us.

For example, it's said that Prussian King Frederick the Great (1712-1786) lost the battle of Jena even though it was fought in 1806. This means that for twenty years after his death, the Prussian army perpetuated his successful organization instead of adapting to meet the changes in the art of war. Had his generals questioned King Frederick's hallowed military tenets, they might have fared better against Napoleon. Similarly, I once read about a group of Russian immigrants in Los Angeles who had the tradition of celebrating New Year's Eve on the afternoon of December 30th. A newspaper reporter asked them, "Why are you celebrating the arrival of the New Year thirty-six hours before everyone else?" One of them, a man in his late sixties, replied, "When we growing up in the Soviet Union forty years ago, we were very poor, and we found that it was a lot cheaper to get a band on the afternoon of the thirtieth. That's how the tradition began." The curious thing is these people had prospered in America and they could easily have afforded lavish entertainment on New Year's Eve, and yet they continued to celebrate it on the previous afternoon.

Another example of this phenomenon (and one appropriate to the river metaphor of this Creative Insight) is the Pike Syndrome so named after experiments performed to test the adaptive behavior of the pike. The pike — a long, lean fish with sharp teeth — is a ferocious predator whose main prey are smaller fish. The experiment was conducted in the following manner: a clear bell jar filled with water and minnows was placed in a large aquarium containing a pike. As would be expected, the pike lunged at the minnows. But each time it did this, it would painfully bang its nose and face. After many attempts, the pike finally ceased his attacks and ignored the minnows. Now, here's the interesting part: the experimenters then removed the bell jar so that the minnows could swim freely — even right in front of the pike — but now the pike would not attack. It had associated pain with the minnows and was unable to adapt to the new reality of an easily accessible, "pain-free" meal. Like Frederick's generals and the early New Year's celebrants, the pike was unable to understand that what he had learned no longer made sense because conditions had changed.

Once a rule, pattern, or behavior is firmly established, it's very difficult to eliminate even though the original reason for it has gone away. Indeed, creative thinking involves not only generating new ideas, but eliminating obsolete ones as well. Thus, when examining an existing rule, program, or policy, it's always a good practice to ask, "Why did this rule come to be?" Then follow this question with, "Do these reasons still exist?" If the answer is "No," then eliminate the rule. ❖ **What assumptions should you update? What's obsolete and can be discarded?**

SEE HOW YOU ARE CHANGED. By stepping into the river, we change both the river and ourselves. Thus, getting involved in a particular situation changes both it and us. For example, when my daughter was in high school, she tutored a hearing-impaired preteen for whom English was a second language. After two years, her student had greatly improved her linguistic skills. Interestingly, my daughter discovered that her own language abilities were also enhanced — specifically her sensitivity to word rhythms and sentence cadences in her own and others' writing.

Similarly, a key insight of modern quantum physics is that by observing a given phenomenon, the observer affects the object being observed. Perhaps this is what Heraclitus had in mind: we're part of the cosmic process, and our participation changes the things with which we interact. Indeed, some physicists have gone so far as to say that any universe that fails to develop conscious life to apprehend its existence never truly existed to begin with! ❖ **How is involvement in your current situation changing both it and you? What are you learning from it?**

"That which opposes produces a benefit."

τὸ ἀντίξουν συμφέρον.

BEWARE OF ROUTINES. Routines are the boon and bane of our existence. They're beneficial because they allow us to get things done without much thought. For example, if every morning you had to relearn how to dress yourself or cook your breakfast, you'd never make it to work on time. Routines can be harmful, however, if they prevent us from developing a fresh perspective. They are most dangerous when we are least conscious of the extent to which our perception and cognition are guided by them. Sometimes our habits become so integral to our thinking that we fail to identify them as habits, and instead consider them "the way things are done." Thus, we need an occasional jolt to shake us out of our mental patterns. I call this jolt "a whack on the side of the head," and it can stimulate us to ask the questions that lead us to new answers.*

Here's an example: suppose that every Saturday afternoon you bake bread following the same

---

*The nineteenth-century German philosopher Friedrich Nietzsche, an admirer of Heraclitus, had similar feelings. In *Twilight of the Idols,* he says*:* "That which does not kill me makes me stronger."

steps as usual. Now, let's further suppose that one Saturday there's an obstacle in your path — a broken oven — that prevents you from reaching your objective. As a result, one of the following might happen: (1) you use your creative abilities to eliminate the obstacle (you fix the oven); (2) you go around the obstacle and find another way to reach your objective (you use a neighbor's oven or go to the store and buy the bread); (3) in the course of the search, you find a new objective that is preferable to the original one (you find a place selling exotic pizza) and that you wouldn't have discovered had you not been forced off the routine path; or, (4) you question whether you even need to reach your objective (you decide to go dancing instead of eating). Thus, opposition — in the form of problems and obstacles — can provide the benefit of forcing us to stop and rethink what we're doing.

Think about it: the history of discovery and invention is filled with people whose routines were disrupted and who were forced to come up with alternative solutions. A very significant but unheralded example of this phenomenon is the search for pepper. As a matter of fact, the spread of Europeans throughout the world after the year 1500 has much to do with the supply of pepper. From the Middle Ages on, pepper was far and away the most important spice traded between Europe and the Far East. That's because no other spice except pepper made heavily salted meat edible, and in Europe no form of preservation other than salting was generally employed. Thus, it was salt and pepper that stood between the carnivorous Europeans and starvation. Around 1470, the Turks began disrupting the overland trade routes east from the Mediterranean. This caused pepper to be in short supply and prices to skyrocket. As a result, European explorers sailed west and south in search of alternative passages to the Orient. As historian Henry Hobson put it, "The Americas were discovered as a by-product in the search for pepper." ❖ **What's creating opposition in your situation? Are there alternative ways to reach your objective? Is the goal you originally sought still desirable? What opportunities would open up if you abandoned it?**

"A wonderful harmony is created when we join together the seemingly unconnected."

άρμονίη άφανὴς φανερῆς κρείττων.

CONNECT THE UNCONNECTED. Making connections is essential to life: it's the basis of invention, poetry, air travel, business success, romance, boxing, communication, humor, intelligence work, and crime detection. As design critic Ralph Caplan put it, "All art, and most knowledge, entails either seeing connections or making them. Until it is hooked up with what you already know, nothing can be learned or assimilated."

Why did Heraclitus consider joining together "the seemingly unconnected" so wonderful? Perhaps he realized that when the same ideas are brought together again and again, they lose their potency and become increasingly predictable. Examples include clichés, jokes with obvious punchlines, overused metaphors, and small talk.

Conversely it is the joining together of previously unconnected ideas that makes us sing out "Aha!" and see things in a fresh way. Indeed, this act of making new connections lies at the heart of the creative process. Inventors combine components to craft new products: Gutenberg joined together the wine press and the coin punch to create moveable type and the printing press. Entrepreneurs bring together resources from different arenas to build new businesses: Joseph Pulitzer added large-scale advertising to high speed printing to create the mass circulation newspaper. Engineers mix different materials to create new ones: ancient Greek metallurgists alloyed soft copper with even softer tin to produce hard bronze.

Artists draw on nature and technology to express new possibilities: architect Frank Gehry combined the scale structure of a fish with advanced aircraft-cutting technology to fashion the titanium skin design of the Bilbao (Spain) Guggenheim Museum. Surrealists link unrelated objects to evoke feelings of confusion and wonder: painter René Magritte depicted a steaming locomotive emerging from the mouth of a dining room fireplace in his work Time Transfixed.

Playful crossword puzzle editors bring together unlikely ideas as clues for the same word: "quick good-bye gesture" and "modern kitchen appliance" both connote "microwave." Scientists marry diverse concepts to give birth to new models of explanation: naturalist Charles Darwin combined the idea of random genetic mutations with natural selection to arrive at his theory of evolution. Poets mix unusual images to create provocative metaphors: Luciano de Crescenzo, "We are all angels with just one wing — we can only fly while embracing each other."

Crime investigators connect disparate evidence to build convincing cases: Sherlock Holmes tied the stolen boot, ancestral portrait, and perfumed stationery to the baronet's murderer in *The Hound of the Baskervilles*. Humorists juxtapose unrelated situations for comic effect: "What do you call a clairvoyant midget who just broke out of prison? A small medium at large!" ❖ **What unconnected ideas can you join together?**

CREATE A METAPHOR. A powerful way to join ideas together is to make a metaphor. You can create this "wonderful harmony" simply by recognizing similarities between unrelated phenomena. Indeed, this is how our thinking grows: we understand the unfamiliar by comparing it to what we know. For example, the first automobiles were called "horse-less carriages." The first locomotives were dubbed "iron horses." We see metaphorical resemblances all around us: appliances have "footprints," cities

have "hearts," modems have "handshake" proto-
cols, tennis racquets have "sweet spots," ideas can be
"half-baked," problems "snowball," and conscious-
ness flows like a "stream."★

Heraclitus enthusiastically employed this technique of using one concept to express another in
many of his epigrams: "barking dogs" for critical
people, "garbage-eating donkeys" for impoverished
value systems, "avenging Furies" for limits, and "blazing fire" for unbridled arrogance.

Of course, many other great teachers have also
used metaphors to express their ideas. Socrates com-
pared the human mind to a "ship in which the sail-
ors had mutinied and locked up the Captain be-

★Speaking of thinking, here is a delicious metaphor for the
mind. In meditation, the meditator wants his mind to be still,
to "mirror" reality much as a "quiet lake reflects the moon."
But this is much easier said than done — the surface is
choppy at best. As religion writer Huston Smith puts it, the
restless mind can be likened to "a crazed monkey cavorting
about its cage. Or rather, a drunken crazed monkey. But more!
— a drunken, crazed monkey that has St. Vitus' Dance. Even this
is insufficient. The mind is like a drunken crazed monkey with
St. Vitus' Dance who has just been stung by a wasp." Those who
have tried to meditate will not find this metaphor extreme.

low." Jesus likened the Kingdom of God to a "hidden treasure" and a "wedding feast." For Buddha, the First Noble Truth is that life is *dukkha* (usually translated as "suffering"). During his time, *dukkha* referred to wheels whose axles were off-center or bones that had slipped from their sockets. Buddha made metaphoric use of this term to stress that life is "out of joint," and "its pivot is not true." Ancient Chinese philosopher Lao-tzu employed the concepts of a "windowless room" and "the empty hub of a thirty-spoked wheel" to describe the ineffable nature of the *Tao*. Solomon used many metaphors in his Proverbs including "clouds and wind without rain" to represent a man who boasts of a gift he does not give, and "a dog that returns to his vomit" to portray a fool who repeats his folly.

How about a metaphor for metaphors? I like to think of them as "maps." In the same way that a map represents a territory's layout and highlights its various sites and roads, metaphors depict the general structure of the ideas they represent. Also, just as different types of maps emphasize different features (that is, political maps highlight information markedly different from topographical or population maps), different metaphors for the same subject can paint quite diverse pictures. For example, here are three metaphors for life. (1) Life is like a jigsaw puzzle but you don't have the picture on the front of the box to use as a guide. Sometimes, you're not even sure if you have all the pieces. (2) Life is like a bagel. It's delicious when it's fresh and warm, but often it's just hard. The hole in the middle is its great mystery, and yet it wouldn't be a bagel without it. (3) Life is like a poker game. You deal or are dealt to. You bet, check, bluff, and raise. You learn from those you play with. Sometimes you win with a pair or lose with a full house. But whatever happens, it's best to keep shuffling along.

Metaphors can also give us a fresh insight into a problem or situation. In the early twentieth century Danish physicist Niels Bohr developed a new model of the atom by comparing it to the solar system. Within this framework, he figured that the sun represented the nucleus and the planets represented electrons. Seventeenth-century British physician William Harvey looked at the heart not as an organ or muscle but as a pump and this led to his conception of the circulation of blood. More recently, American biologist Leigh Van Valen was inspired by the Red Queen character from Lewis Carroll's *Through the Looking Glass*. (She's the one who runs hard but never gets anywhere because everything else in the landscape is also running. As she tells Alice, "It takes all the running you can do to keep in the same place!") Van Valen used the Red Queen as a metaphor for his evolutionary principle that regardless of how well a species adapts to its current environment, it must keep evolving in order to keep up with its competitors and enemies who are also evolving. Thus the "Red Queen Effect": do nothing and fall behind, or run hard to stay where you are. (This is also found in business, new technology development, and arms races.)

Try making a metaphor for a current problem. Simply compare your situation to something else and then see what similarities you can find between the ideas. Tip: often the most fertile metaphors are those in which there is some action taking place. ❖ **What metaphors can you create for your issue? Conducting an orchestra? Cultivating a garden? Waging war? Raising a child? Selling a product? Planning a vacation?**

"If all things turned to smoke, the nose would become the discerning organ."

εἰ πάντα τὰ ὄντα καπνὸς γένοιτο, ῥῖνες ἂν διαγνοῖεν.

ALTER YOUR STRATEGY. "Things turning to smoke" represents a dramatic change of conditions. The nose becoming the "discerning organ" represents an equally dramatic response to that situation. So Heraclitus is saying, "If the idea you're working on were burnt to a crisp, would you be able to sniff out an opportunity in its ashes and vapors?"

An example of where this happened is the Great Fire of Rome in 64 C.E. (during Nero's reign). In the fire's aftermath, officials realized that to prevent future conflagrations, they needed to rethink their basic construction methods. The result was that they radically upgraded their building codes — for example, the use of wood in beams was discouraged. These changes allowed the widespread use of a relatively new building material: pozzolana-enriched concrete.* This flexible material freed Roman architects from constraints such as right angles and allowed them to develop new shapes such as the

---

*Concrete, made of mud, mortar, and adobe, had been a building material for millennia. The Romans, however, discovered that by adding a new material to the mix, the volcanic mineral pozzolana, their concrete would be stronger and dry faster.

dome and the vault. Here, the catastrophe of the fire served as a catalyst for architectural change. ❖ **If your situation were greatly transformed, could you let go of the past and adopt new ways of thinking?**

ASK "WHAT IF?" Heraclitus proposed a hypothetical situation and then imagined the implications of it. This is the formula for asking "what if" questions and discovering new possibilities. What if people had edible clothing? Perhaps fashions would change as different foods came into season. What if men also had babies? Social-welfare laws might be structured quite differently. What if the earth had no moon? Our planet's tilt would be less consistent, thus greatly increasing the likelihood of climate instability. What if you had an "entropy meter" to measure the amount of order and disorder around you? You could use it to help you find just the right amount of stimulation or serenity you needed in your life. What if human beings always told the truth? Living in a world where you knew exactly what others thought of you could lead to more honest relationships. It could also cause more people to suffer mental breakdowns.

In my opinion, one of the most important "what if" questions ever asked was posed in the eighth-century B.C.E. by an anonymous Greek scribe looking for ways to improve the reading process. A little background: At that time, the Greek alphabet — like previous alphabets such as the Phoenician (on which the Greek one was based) and the Hebrew — consisted of only consonants, no vowels. This writing system made reading a slow and imprecise process. To understand a word, the reader had to guess the missing vowel sounds between consonants to correctly grasp the meaning. For example, a modern English equivalent might be: does the two-consonant word "bd" stand for "bad," "bed," "bid," "bud," or even "abide"? As with most other cognitive activities, context and experience would be the guides to the proper interpretation.

Much of creative thinking involves looking at the same thing as everyone else and thinking something different. And that's what this innovative scribe did. As he pondered the alphabet before him, the "what if" question he must have asked himself was: "What if I looked at these symbols in a different way, and let some of the letters represent the vowel sounds we actually speak rather than just consonants? What would be possible?" The eventual result was the creation of seven written vowels (*alpha, epsilon, eta, iota, omicron, upsilon,* and *omega*). By combining these with the existing consonants, he — and other scribes of the period who contributed to and adopted this convention — created the first fully phonetic alphabet.

This is a truly powerful invention! A fully phonetic alphabet — that is, one capable of expressing all of the spoken sounds in a language — enabled writers to translate spoken words exactly into written ones, and readers to do the opposite. This system also increased the reader's speed and comprehension. The fact that children could easily learn this new system certainly contributed to its success. Thus, with the addition of vowels, these early Greeks both simplified and gave new power to writing and reading. Considering the importance of language to our thinking processes, it is difficult to understate the significance of this development. ❖ **What imaginative "what if" questions can you ask? What if you knew that you had only three months left to live? What decisions would you make?**

SWITCH SENSES. There is a great variety of information available to us — visual, auditory, tactile, intuitive, olfactory,★ etc. — but often we dwell on only a small portion of it. Heraclitus encourages us to exercise all of our senses as a way of stimulating our thinking. For example, suppose you're visiting an auto assembly plant. In addition to noting the various steps in which the vehicle is put together, you might also pay special attention to the sights and smells of large-scale car fabrication. Suppose you're in a fragrant vegetable garden on a summer morning. What sounds do you hear from the growing plants? ❖ **What other senses can you use in your current situation?**

★Relevant to Heraclitus' insight are naturalist Diane Ackerman's comments about smell: "Early in our evolution, smell was essential. Many forms of sea life must sit and wait for food to brush up against them or stray within their tentacled grasp. But, guided by smell, we became nomads who could go out and search for food, hunt it, even choose what we're hankering for. Smell was the first of our senses, and it was so successful that in time the small lump of olfactory tissue atop the nerve cord grew into a brain. Our cerebral hemispheres were originally buds from the olfactory stalks. We *think* because we *smelled*."

"The Sun will not exceed its limits, because the avenging Furies, ministers of Justice, would find out."

῎Ηλιος γὰρ οὐχ ὑπερβήσεται μέτρα· εἰ᾽ δὲ μή,
᾽Ερινύες μιν Δίκης ἐπίκουροι ἐξευρήσουσιν.

LET FURIES BECOME MUSES. For the cosmos to be "ordered," most things have set limits within which they must function. For example, the sun must rise in the east, set in the west, travel close to the horizon in winter, and be nearer the meridian in summer. If it rose in the west or remained stationary for hours at a time, there would be chaos. Heraclitus uses the mytho-religious metaphor of the "avenging Furies" for the horrific force that prevents things from overstepping their bounds.

But fear not! Strict limits can be a powerful stimulant to the creative process. If you've ever been asked to solve a challenging problem with a small budget or a tight deadline, you've probably found that you were much more resourceful than if you had been granted a ton of money and time. As architect Frank Lloyd Wright repeatedly told his students, "Limits are an artist's best friend." That's because they force us to think beyond conventional solutions and find answers we might not otherwise have discovered.

For example, skyscrapers were not developed by people with cheap, unlimited land, but rather by innovators who wrestled with the problem, "How do we create abundant office space on small pieces of expensive real estate?" Another example: Islamic artists were (and are) generally forbidden by the Koran to depict images of the human body and recognizable life forms in their work. As a result, they channeled their passion for form into representing the geometrical patterns that can be found in the natural world. Their ingenuity is especially evident in the Alcazar and Alhambra palaces in Spain, where fourteenth-century Moorish designers crafted intricate symmetries in their wall and floor mosaics. Interestingly, six centuries later physicists determined that there are thirty-two different ways in which the atoms and molecules in a crystal can be symmetrically arranged in a pattern — and these are all represented in the Moorish mosaics!

Similarly, a poet may be more inspired by the challenge of writing a sonnet, which must follow a standard pattern of rhyme and meter, than by writing free verse.* Indeed, some people enjoy adding

---

*As poet Robert Frost put it, "Writing free verse is like playing tennis without a net."

constraints to their problems as a way of spurring their thinking. Composer Stephen Sondheim says: "If you ask me to write a song about the ocean, I'm stumped. But if you tell me to write a ballad about a woman in a red dress falling off her stool at three in the morning, I'm inspired." ❖ **How can you turn the constraints of your situation to your advantage? What limits can you add to your problem?**

THINK ABOUT THE CONSEQUENCES. When we alter something (for example, the dynamics of a personal relationship, the wording of a classic advertising slogan, or the compensation system of the military), forces may be set in motion that lead to undesired results (your spouse leaves, sales decline, or the army revolts). It is fear of these consequences (the Furies) that prevents some of us from changing things in the first place. ❖ **What Furies hold you in check? What havoc would be wrought if you changed something that seems "unalterable"?**

"Lovers of wisdom must open their minds to very many things."

χρὴ γὰρ εὖ μάλα πολλῶν ἵστορας
φιλοσόφους ἄνδρας εἶναι.

BE AN EXPLORER. To create new ideas, we need the materials from which they're made: knowledge, feeling, information, and experience. We can look for these in the same old places. However, we're much more likely to find something original if we venture off the beaten path.

Indeed, many good ideas have been discovered because someone poked around in an outside industry or discipline, and applied what he found to his own field or problem. Mathematician John von Neumann analyzed poker-table behavior to create the "game theory" model of economics. Nineteenth-century English gardener Joseph Paxton modeled his design of the world's first glass-and-iron building, the Crystal Palace, on his studies of the cantilevered rib structure of the giant water lily *Victoria amazonica*.

Designer Charles Eames borrowed from his experience crafting custom-fitted plywood splints for wounded airmen during World War II to create a new line of aesthetically stunning chairs. Physicist Albert Einstein applied the non-Euclidean geometry of nineteenth-century mathematician Georg Riemann to represent his four-dimensional map of light.

Database developer Erik Lumer created a more flexible customer-profiling system for the banking industry by studying how worker ants cluster their dead when cleaning their nests. Biochemist Stephen Fodor employed the photolithography masking techniques used in semiconductor manufacturing to create the DNA microarray tools that have revolutionized gene analysis. And World War I military designers borrowed from the cubist art of Picasso and Braque to create more efficient camouflage patterns. I've known advertising people who got ideas from biology, software programmers who received inspiration from songwriters, and investors who spotted new opportunities by going to junkyards.

A good explorer has the attitude that there's a lot of valuable information available, and all he has to do is find it. Here's a tip: open your mind up to things that have no connection with the problem you're trying to solve. Indeed, the more divergent your sources, the more original the idea you create is likely to be. If you go to an airport, you'll find ideas there. If you go to a museum, you'll find ideas there too. And the same applies to hardware stores, garbage dumps, circuses, libraries, political rallies, and wilderness areas. As inventor Thomas Edison told his colleagues: "Make it a practice to be on the lookout for novel and interesting ideas that others have used successfully. Your idea has to be original only in its adaptation to the problem you're working on." ❖ **Where do you rarely look for ideas? What might you find if you went there?**

STAY CURIOUS. Curiosity may have killed a lot of cats, but asking questions is the best way to learn about anything. Leonardo da Vinci said, "I roamed the countryside searching for answers to things I did not understand. Why shells exist on the tops of mountains along with imprints of plants usually found in the sea. Why thunder lasts longer than that which causes it. How circles of water form around a spot that has been struck by a stone. And how a bird suspends itself in the air. Questions like these engaged my thought throughout my life." ❖ **What are you curious about?**

"I searched into myself."

ἐδιζησάμην ἐμεωυτόν.

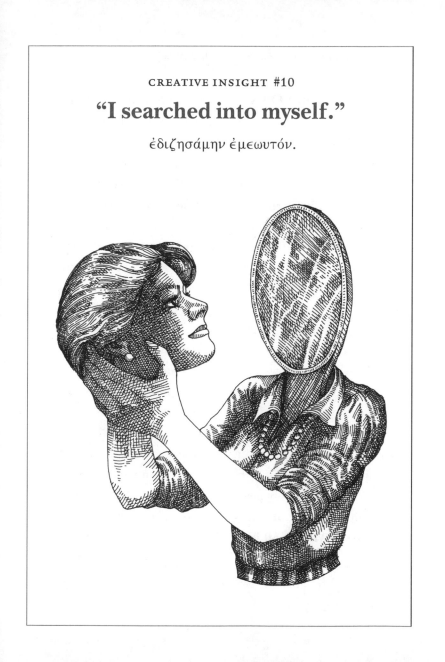

UNLOCK YOUR OWN ANSWERS. Heraclitus felt that consulting our own experience and intuition is a wonderful way to gain insight. Unfortunately, some of us have never learned this lesson. Much of our educational system is an elaborate game of "guess what the teacher is thinking," and we come to believe that the best ideas are in someone else's head rather than our own. Heraclitus reminds us that there are good ideas within ourselves if we are willing to dig deep enough.

Sometimes our own attitudes can prevent us from accessing these ideas. I call the attitudes that imprison our thinking "mental locks." They include such beliefs as "There is one right answer," "Always be practical," "Follow the rules," "That's not my area," "Avoid ambiguity," and "Don't be foolish." These attitudes make sense in some situations, but they tend to interfere when we're trying to be creative. One technique I use for opening mental locks is to do the opposite — that is, I try to look for more than one right answer, worry less about how correct I am, seek inspiration in outside areas, embrace paradox, and so on. ❖ **What good ideas do you have waiting for expression? What mental locks keep you from gaining access to them? How can you open them?**

FIND YOUR OWN CREATIVE TENDENCIES. We can emulate Heraclitus by searching for our own creative characteristics. Here are ten of mine:

1. I get my ideas either when I'm under a lot of pressure (the ultimate inspiration is the deadline) or when I'm away from a problem altogether. I rarely get them when I'm doing routine tasks that require some attention. Also, I can sometimes come up with a good idea on demand. But I'm more likely to do so when I've had an opportunity to sleep on the issue.

2. If I'm mentally blocked in trying to solve a problem, it's usually because I'm in love with a particular idea — so much so that it prevents me from looking for alternatives. Only when I force myself to become detached from it and "kiss it goodbye" do I find new answers. Letting go of a previously cherished idea can be one of life's great pleasures.

3. I try to pay attention to small things: how frequently pentagons appear in nature, how much frowning takes place in beer commercials, what sorts of patterns dead leaves and other debris make around a storm drain, and so on. I do this partly because I've trained myself to do it, but also be-

cause I've been forced to. I'm left-handed, but the world is designed for right-handed people — something most "righties" don't even think about. I'm constantly being made conscious of how things are put together. For example, telephone booths are designed to make right-handed people comfortable and at ease, but lefties can feel clumsy using them.

4. My own ego can get in the way of discovering new things. However, if I allow myself to lower my resistance to those ideas that I typically dismiss as irrelevant or unattractive, I find that they can become doorways to solutions I've been overlooking.

5. A dose of ambiguity stimulates my imagination. When I'm confused about a situation, I'm more likely to consider unusual options and explanations that just might help me solve my problem. Confusion is disorienting but I also know that it's a sign I'm making progress.

6. I love metaphors! Their imagery lights up my mind. If given the choice between an in-depth analysis of a situation or a vivid metaphor for the same, I'll usually opt for the latter. Indeed, some of my best ideas have started out as metaphors. The

image that came to me early on for Heraclitus' epigrams was "jewels of insight." After all, I considered them small and valuable. Like jewels, each one has many facets, some of which catch more light than others.

7. I don't know what I don't know. I've got a big blind spot, and the only way to get access to what's lurking there is to put myself in a humble, receptive frame of mind (not always easy to do) and ask others to point out what I'm not seeing.

8. Rejection of my work in the early stages of the creative process doesn't bother me. I'm not afraid of taking one of my less-than-stellar ideas and asking complete strangers what they think of it. I find their responses frank and refreshing.

9. I like "playing the fool" as a means of stirring up my own and others' thinking. I don't mind making an "out-of-left-field" comment to see what reaction it generates. Or asking the stupid question that nobody else seems to be asking.

10. Finally, I believe that there are four roles we adopt during different phases of the creative process: explorer, artist, judge, and warrior. I feel that I'm a pretty good "explorer," that is, I'm able

to get off the beaten path and find information in outside areas. I'm a fairly decent "artist," that is, I'm good at playing with ideas and turning them into something new. I'm a more than an adequate "warrior," that is, I'm able to champion an idea and get it into action.* My weakest role is my "judge"; my ability to evaluate the critical merits of an idea could be better. ❖ **What's your creative thinking style? How do you get your ideas? What are your strengths? Weaknesses?**

---

*How would you rate your four creative roles? **1. How venturesome is your explorer?** (a) My friends call me "ostrich head"; (b) I see only what's in front of me; (c) I make time to explore; (d) "Go and find it" is my middle name; or (e) Columbus, Madame Curie, and the Apollo space program all rolled into one! **2. How imaginative is your artist?** (a) my imagination's in prison; (b) I can follow a recipe; (c) I'm usually good for a new insight; (d) part magician, part poet, part child; or (e) Picasso and Mozart, make room! **3. How discerning is your judge?** (a) I don't understand decision-making; (b) flipping a coin would get better results; (c) I can usually pick out what's worth building on in a new idea; (d) I'm right more often than not; or (e) I have the wisdom of Solomon! **4. How persistent is your warrior?** (a) I'm a real wimp; (b) I'm fine until I hit an excuse or two; (c) I get up when I'm knocked down; (d) I get things done; or (e) I'm in the ranks of Caesar and Patton!

CREATIVE INSIGHT #11

"Knowing many things doesn't teach insight."

πολυμαθίη νόον οὐ διδάσκει.

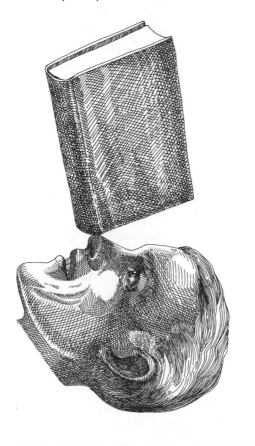

BE ARTFUL WITH YOUR KNOWLEDGE. We've all known people who knew many things but who never did anything very innovative with their learning. Heraclitus realized that the key to being more creative is being able to work and play with our knowledge. Using our knowledge is a lot like cooking. Getting a satisfying result depends on what things we add together and how we mix them.

For example, suppose we assigned each of a dozen cooks the task of preparing an interesting dish with the following ingredients: chicken, tomatoes, spinach, eggplant, potatoes, honey, ginger, oregano, and raisins. Some might make a salad, others a soup or a stew, and still others an *hors d'oeuvre* or perhaps even a dessert. Some of the dishes might be delicious, and others barely edible. Also, some cooks will closely follow a recipe while others might be a bit more imaginative — say, dyeing the soup purple. (One cook might even have the nerve to eat all the ingredients himself and then tell us, "Today you should fast!") The point is that with the same resources, different people will come up with different solutions — some more successful than others.

Outside the kitchen, life is no different. Like cooks forced to improvise, we must draw on everything we know in order to achieve success, even if our experiments sometimes fail. Whether it's repairing an automobile engine, coaching a team of little leaguers, selling a new product to a demanding customer, or counseling a friend during a time of loss, we must decide (1) which of our ideas to emphasize and *which to ignore*; (2) what to interpret literally and *what to take as a metaphor*; (3) when to apply a principle and *when to disregard it*; and finally, (4) when to let an idea stand on its own and *when to connect it with other ideas*. Thus, creative insight arises not just from having knowledge, but from being able to work and play with this knowledge. ❖ **What ideas should you focus on in your current situation? What might you ignore? Are there some ideas that should be viewed metaphorically rather than literally — or vice versa?**

PRACTICE FORGETTING. Forgetting what we know — at the appropriate time — can be an important means for gaining insight. This is illustrated in the story about a creativity teacher who invited a student to his house for afternoon tea. They talked for a while, and then it was teatime. The teacher poured some tea into the student's cup. Even after the cup was full, he continued to pour, and soon tea overflowed onto the floor. Finally, the student said, "You must stop pouring; the tea isn't going into the cup." The teacher replied, "The same is true with you. If you are to receive any of my teachings, you must first empty out the contents of your mental cup." His point: without the ability to forget, our minds remain cluttered with ready-made answers, and we are not motivated to ask the questions that lead our thinking to new ideas.

For example, one day, on his regular walk past the local blacksmith's workshop on the island of Samos, the ancient Greek philosopher Pythagoras temporarily forgot that the banging sounds produced by the smith's hammering of iron bars were "noise" — his usual reaction — and instead viewed them as "information." He soon discovered that musical pitch is a function of the length of the material being struck — his first principle of mathematical physics. Remember: everyone has the ability to forget. The art is knowing when to use it. Indeed, novelist Henry Miller once stated that his "forgettery" was just as important to his success as his memory.

One good way to practice forgetting is with "lateral thinking" puzzles, which require us to let go of our initial assumptions in order to solve them. Here is a classic example of this genre: "John and Mary are lying dead on the floor and there is broken glass and water all around them. How did they die?" Many people assume that the description is of a murder scene. Were they poisoned or shot to death? Perhaps they were stabbed with broken glass. Others may assume there was an accident, or perhaps that a hurricane has drowned them. These explanations are plausible given the information provided. The catch is that John and Mary are two goldfish whose bowl has been accidentally knocked to the floor. Only people who are able to "forget" their assumptions that John and Mary are human beings can find the solution. Here are some lateral thinking puzzles for you to practice and develop your forgetting skills! (1) Five beautiful and well-dressed women are standing in a tight group. One is crying and she's never been happier. The other four are smiling and they have never been more disappointed. What is going on? (2) One morning, a woman rushes into an exclusive art gallery and does grave damage to several of the gallery's most expensive paintings. That afternoon, instead of being arrested, she is given a reward by the gallery's owner. Why? (3) Franz is guilty of no crime, and yet he is surrounded by four uniformed men, one of whom hits him until he cries. Why? (4) Seymour and Irving are lumberjacks. They both work at exactly the same rate. Seymour works nonstop from nine in the morning until five in the afternoon. Irving also works the same hours but he takes a ten minute break every hour. At the end of each day, Irving cuts down many more trees than Seymour. Why? ❖ **What conventional wisdom are you relying on in your situation? What would happen if you forgot the obvious answers that spring to mind and searched for new ones? What can you overlook or ignore?**

"Many fail to grasp what's right in the palm of their hand."

ᾧ μάλιστα διηνεκῶς ὁμιλοῦσι τούτῳ διαφέρονται.

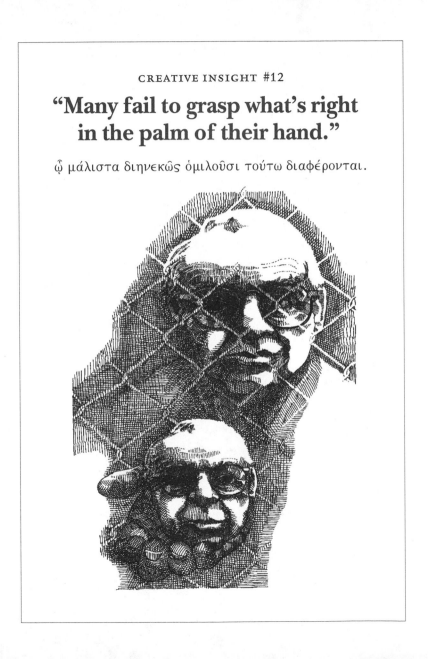

SEE THE WONDER. As children, we are awestruck by most of life. Everyday events — from the chirp of a cricket to a telephone conversation with faraway relatives — seem nothing less than miraculous to the average three-year-old. Yet somehow, as we grow into adulthood, that sense of wonderment gets drummed out of us. Too many of us sleepwalk through our lives, focusing on trivial matters ("that car took my parking place") and get locked into narrow ways of thinking ("my way is the right way").

Heraclitus' advice is to wake up to the wonders of our existence. What amazing things do you grasp? That the sun rose this morning and you're alive to enjoy it? That plants contain the pigment chlorophyll that allows them to store the sun's energy? That ingredients in the bark of the cinchona tree can combat the deadly effects of malaria? That your car brakes work virtually every time you use them? That compassion between human beings isn't all that rare? That wind chimes evoke childhood memories of spring rain? As scientist Lewis Thomas put it, "Statistically, the probability of any one of us being here is so small that the mere fact of our existence should keep us all in a state of contented dazzlement." ❖ **Do you see the magic in what you're doing? What deadens your awareness of things? What heightens it?**

SEE THE OBVIOUS. Sometimes the most helpful ideas are right in front of us, but we fail to see them. For example, if you study the evolution of the bicycle during the 1860s and 1870s, you will notice that both wheels started out at about the same size. Over time, however, the front wheel got larger and larger, and the rear wheel became significantly smaller. The reason was that initially the pedals were attached directly to the front wheel. Since there was no drive train on the bicycle, the only way to make the bike go faster was to make the front wheel bigger. The culmination of this trend was the "penny farthing" model with a front wheel almost 1.5 meters in diameter. Needless to say, such bicycles weren't very safe.

The curious thing about this whole development is that the solution for a better and safer bicycle was right in front of the bicycle designers. The bicycles themselves were manufactured using drive-train technology! Finally, someone looked up and made the obvious connection, and asked, "Why not use a drive train to power the rear wheel?" Within only a few years this safer model supplanted the penny farthing. Remember: nothing evades our attention quite so persistently as that which we take for granted. ❖ **What resources are right in front of you? If you step back away from your situation, what are the most obvious things you can say about it?**

CREATIVE INSIGHT #13

"When there is no sun,
we can see the evening stars."

εἰ μὴ ἥλιος ἦν, ἕνεκα τῶν
ἄλλων ἄστρων εὐφρόνη ἂν ἦν.

LOOK FOR THE STARS. In this wonderful metaphor, the "sun" represents the dominant feature of a thing or situation. Here are a few examples: a person who overshadows a group, a noise that drowns out other sounds, a strong spice that overwhelms the other flavors in a food dish, a player who outshines his teammates, an activity that leaves no time to do anything else, or the conventional way of solving a particular problem. The "evening stars" represent the less obvious aspects of a situation. We don't see them because the "sun" is so bright. But when there is no sun, these "stars" are visible. To say this in another way: discovery often means the uncovering of something that was always there but was obscured by something else.

The following apocryphal story is an example of this. One day in the fourth century B.C.E., an anonymous Greek librarian had the task of storing away a large number of manuscripts that had recently come into his possession. He asked himself: "What simple ordering system can I devise for these works so that I — or anyone else — can easily retrieve them later?" After playing with the issue for a while, he thought of the Greek alphabet

— but not as it was usually conceived. His contemporaries typically considered the alphabet to be a series of phonetic symbols with names (*alpha, beta, gamma, delta, epsilon, zeta* . . .) that were used primarily to form words that conveyed meaning, or less often to represent numbers. The librarian decided to de-emphasize the alphabet's linguistic and numerical functions. By doing so, he was able to focus on a less apparent feature: each letter's relationship to the others in the alphabet. He thought: "If I place those manuscripts whose titles begin with *beta* before those beginning with *gamma* but after those beginning with *alpha*, and use that same logic throughout, I'll create a storage and retrieval system that's simple and efficient." And that's what he did. By consciously ignoring the alphabet's "sun" (its linguistic function), the librarian was able to discover the "stars" of alphabetization. ❖ **What's the most dominant feature of your situation? What new "stars" come into view when you ignore this feature? Is your ego the "sun" that outshines other possibilities? What would happen if you let it be eclipsed?**

GET AWAY FROM THE PROBLEM. Sometimes turning a problem over to the active powers of our unconscious can be a good technique for gaining a new perspective. As software designer Rick Tendy puts it, "I never try to solve a problem by trying to solve it."

The classic example of this strategy involved Archimedes, the third-century B.C.E. Greek mathematician and ballistic weapons designer. He was asked by the tyrant Hiero of Syracuse to determine the purity of a gold crown suspected of being adulterated with silver by the crown's goldsmith. Archimedes knew the weight per volume unit of gold, but since the crown was a holy object, he ruled out solutions such as melting it or hammering it into a measurable cube. After several frustrating weeks of being unable to find an answer, Archimedes decided to get away from the problem altogether by going to the public baths. There he watched absent-mindedly while the water rose with the immersion of his body in the tub. Suddenly inspiration dawned: why not use the same immersion process with the crown? Because gold is denser than silver, he realized that it would displace less water than the lighter metal, that is, the water would not rise as high for a solid gold crown as for one containing silver. It was this solution that led him to run through the streets yelling "Eureka!" ❖ **Have you considered taking a break from a current problem? What diversion might relax you and free your thinking?**

APPRECIATE THE SUN. However beautiful, mysterious, or romantic the evening stars might be, the night, a time when we miss the sun, can also be cold, scary, and dangerous. In other words, we often don't appreciate something until it's gone. Just as the sun provides us with much of the heat, light, and energy that we use to carry on the business of living, the dominant feature of a situation (the "sun" in our metaphor) contributes much to that situation's order and cohesion. Indeed, an imperfect (that is, domineering or overbearing) sun that creates stability is often preferable to no sun at all (chaos or indecision).

For example, even though the Roman Empire was flawed by its many excesses, cruelties, and inequities — especially in its latter stages — it could still boast of a high rate of literacy and a sophisticated legal system. These were lost after its destruction (in the West) by the Vandals, Visigoths, and other barbarian forces. ❖ **What positive things can you say about the dominant feature of your situation? What might be lost without it?**

"The most beautiful order is a heap of sweepings piled up at random."

σάρμα εἰκῆ κεχυμένον ὁ κάλλιστος ὁ κόσμος.

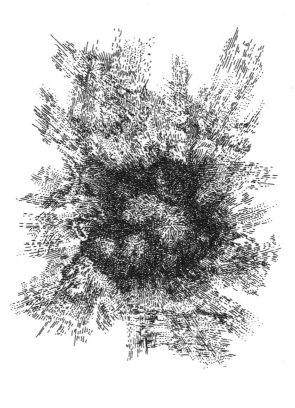

FIND MEANING IN RANDOM IDEAS. Take advantage of your mind's ability to recognize patterns. If it can find meaning — or even beauty — in something as humble as "a heap of random sweepings," you may discover meaning in other places where none is intended. This is borne out in a story about an Indian medicine man who made hunting maps for his tribe. He made them in a unique way. When game got sparse, he'd put a piece of fresh leather in the sun to dry; then he'd fold and twist it, and then smooth it out. The rawhide was now etched with lines. He marked some reference points, and a new map was created. When the hunters followed each new map's "trails," they usually discovered abundant game. By letting the rawhide's random folds represent trails, the medicine man pointed the hunters to places where they hadn't looked before.

We can stimulate our thinking in a similar way by opening our minds up to things that have nothing to do with our current situation. Throw together stuff from different places and you'll find some sort of pattern that has some bearing on what you're doing. Look at the bark of a nearby tree.

What shapes do you see? A map of Europe? Your uncle's profile? Pick out the tenth word on page 204 of your dictionary. How does it relate to what you're doing? Look out your window and find the first thing that has red in it. How does it relate to a problem you're trying to solve? Open a magazine and select the eighth full-page advertisement from the front. How does the product displayed relate to what you're doing? Think of a sport or recreational activity that begins with the same letter as your last name. How does it relate to what you're doing? Open the obituary section of the New York Times and read the first two "obits." What from these people's lives can you apply to your situation? Turn to page 18 of this book and select a number at random. How does the Creative Insight that corresponds to it relate to your situation? ❖ **What patterns can you find in random ideas? How can you connect them to the problem you're trying to solve?**

FIND BEAUTY IN THE MUNDANE. It's not difficult to find beauty in the sublime or the artfully crafted. But Heraclitus challenges us to find it also in the mundane, humble patterns of everyday life — perhaps in the shapes and colors of rust on a sink pipe, or in concentric sweat stains on a dress shirt, or in an empty plastic bag being blown about by the wind, or possibly in snaking lines of people heading to a sold-out event. Doing this not only forces us to reassess the criteria by which we decide what is beautiful, it also requires us — because of the ephemeral nature of many of these phenomena — to focus on the here and now. ❖ **What is humbly beautiful in your current situation?**

"Things love to conceal their true nature."

φύσις κρύπτεσθαι φιλεῖ.

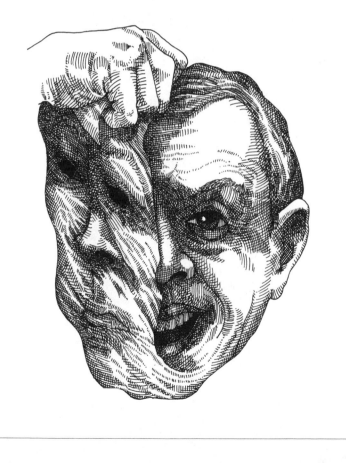

DIG DEEPER. Heraclitus believed that reality is an enigma. But he also believed that this enigma can be understood, and that the key is to find different ways of thinking about it. One strategy is to ask questions that elicit more than one answer. When confronted with a problem, many of us ask: "What's the answer?" as if only one were possible. If, instead, we try asking, "What are the *answers?*" we'll dig more deeply and may come closer to uncovering what we're looking for.* As chemist Linus Pauling put it, "The best way to get a good idea is to get a lot of ideas." For example, what's an automobile? A personal transportation vehicle. A place to conceive ideas and children. A cause of pollution, congestion, and trade imbalance. A source of tax revenues. What else? ❖ **What's the second right answer in your situation?**

---

*Looking for the second right answer is especially important when dealing with ambiguous messages. In 546 B.C.E., Croesus, the last ruler of the Lydian Empire, consulted the Delphic Oracle for ideas on how to deal with the Persians. He received the following prophecy: "If you attack, a great empire will be destroyed." Croesus took this as an encouraging sign, and led his army against the Persian leader Cyrus fully expecting to destroy the Persian Empire. Instead, he was soundly defeated, and it was *his* empire that was lost.

BE ALERT FOR DECEPTION. Deception is an omnipresent part of life. We see it in nature (animals camouflaging themselves for protection against predators; predators disguising their intentions in order to trap their prey), war (a military leader not showing his strength in order to lure an enemy into battle), sports (a team disguising one play as another to confuse the opponent), politics (candidates hiding character flaws), and riddles* (a puzzler deluding would-be solvers with extraneous information and misleading assumptions). ❖ **Is it possible that someone has disguised his intentions from you? What might they be? In what ways are you deceiving yourself?**

---

*In another epigram, Heraclitus suggests that one way to solve a riddle is to see the obvious; however, he also acknowledges that this is easier said than done: **"People fail to recognize the obvious, much in the way that Homer (wisest of all the Greeks) failed to realize that when some boys told him, 'What we saw and caught we left behind, while what we did not see or catch we took away with us,' they were referring to lice."** Having said that, here are four quick riddles for you. (1) How can you carry water in a sieve? (2) How many monkeys can you put in an empty barrel? (3) What is raised in Italy during the rainy season? (4) What has rivers but no water, cities but no buildings, and forests but no trees?

CLEAR YOUR MIND. If "things love to conceal their true nature," perhaps Heraclitus' intended meaning is the opposite of the words themselves. Perhaps things *aren't* all that difficult to understand. Perhaps the main obstacles are our own preconceptions and imagined truths. Maybe he is suggesting that if we can drop our assumptions, we'll come up with fresh solutions.

For example, in 332 B.C.E., the Macedonian general Alexander the Great and his army wintered in the Asian city of Gordium. While there he heard about the town's famous "Gordian Knot." A prophecy stated that whoever undid this strangely complicated knot would become king of Asia. Intrigued by this story, Alexander asked if he could have a try. After fruitless attempts to find the rope-ends, he was stymied. Then he took a moment to clear his mind and realized that the knot was in fact just a mass to be cleaved. He pulled out his sword and sliced it in half. Asia would become his.

❖ **What assumptions have you made about your current situation? What new information might be revealed if you dropped these assumptions?**

"Those who approach life like a child playing a game, moving and pushing pieces, possess the power of kings."

αἰὼν παῖς ἐστι παίζων,
πεσσεύων· παιδὸς ἡ βασιληίη.

PLAY WITH PROBLEMS. "The power of kings" means having mastery over a situation. According to Heraclitus, this power comes from having an attitude similar to that of a child playing a game. This attitude allows you to play with the issue at hand, to "push and move" its various pieces, so as to find out what works and what doesn't. As artist Jasper Johns said when asked to describe what was involved in the creative process: "It's simple, you just take something and then you do something to it, and then you do something else to it. Keep doing this and pretty soon you've got something."

This idea is reflected in one of my favorite print ads, which was created in the 1960s by Charles Piccirillo to promote National Library Week. The headline consisted of the alphabet in lower-case letters like so: **abcdefghijklmnopqrstuvwxyz.** It was followed by this copy: "At your public library they have these arranged in ways that can make you cry, giggle, love, hate, wonder, ponder, and understand. It's astonishing to see what these twenty-six little marks can do. In Shakespeare's hands they became H*amlet.* Mark Twain wound them into *Huckleberry Finn.* James Joyce twisted them into *Ulysses.*

Gibbon pounded them into *The Decline and Fall of the Roman Empire.* John Milton shaped them into *Paradise Lost.*" The ad went on to extol the virtues of reading and mention that good books are available at your library. There are several messages here, but to me the most important is that creative ideas come from manipulating your resources — no matter how few and simple they are. With this outlook, we try different approaches, first one, then another, often not getting anywhere. We use foolish and impractical ideas as stepping stones to practical new ideas. We even break the rules occasionally. ❖ **How can you play with the various parts of your situation? What can you add? Remove? Combine? Invert? Simplify?**

HAVE FUN. One of play's products is fun — a very powerful motivator. For example, Rosalind Franklin, the scientist whose crystallography research was instrumental in the discovery of the structure of DNA, was asked why she pursued her studies. She replied: "Because our work is so much fun!" Similarly, Murray Gell-Mann, the physicist who coined the subatomic term "quark" after a line in James Joyce's

Finnegans Wake,★ was asked to comment on the names of the various types of quarks — "flavor," "color," "charm," "strange," etc. He said: "The terms are just for fun. There's no particular reason to use pompous names. One might as well be playful."†

Finally, the renowned chair designer Bill Stumpf was asked what criteria he uses to select new furniture projects. He responded, "There are three things I look for in my work: I hope to learn something, I want to make some money, and I'd like to have some fun. If the project doesn't have the promise of satisfying at least two of these, I don't sign on." ❖ **How can you make your situation more fun?**

★Joyce himself was a very playful writer. He once mused that "Gee each owe tea eye spells fish." What he was saying was the letters "G," "H," "O," "T," and "I" spell fish. How is this so? If you pronounce "GH" as it is in "rough," "O" as it is in "women," and "TI" as in "motion," it follows that "GHOTI" must be pronounced "fish."

†More recently, fruit-fly geneticists have taken to giving fun names to specific fruit-fly (*Drosophila*) genes. Here are some examples of their genetic nomenclature: "dunce," "radical fringe," "cheap date," "dissatisfaction," and "amnesiac."

LAUGH AT IT. Where do you find a dog with no legs? Where you left him! What's worse than finding a worm in your apple? Finding half a worm! What's the difference between a dancer and a duck? One is quick on her legs, and the other goes "quack" on her eggs! Humor is a lot of fun. But that's not all! There's a close relationship between the "ha-ha" of humor and the "Aha!" of discovery. If you can laugh at a problem or situation, perhaps you'll overturn a few assumptions and come up with some fresh ideas. Indeed, the mental strategies underlying humor — for example, combining different ideas, asking unusual "what if" questions, parodying the rules — are congruent with effective problem-solving techniques.

From my own experience conducting creativity seminars, I've discovered that humor helps to stimulate the flow of ideas. If, early in a session, I encourage the participants to be humorous and off-beat in their approach to the exercises I give them, their answers are generally more interesting and provocative. In addition, they're more creative in their approach to the serious issues that I subsequently present to them. If, on the other hand, I don't use humor, the participants are much more likely to sit on their hands and be judgmental.★

As physicist Niels Bohr once put it, "There are some things that are so serious that you have to laugh at them." Chinese philosopher Lao-tzu expressed a similar sentiment: "As soon as you have made a thought, laugh at it." ❖ **What humorous things can you say about your situation? What strikes you as really funny?**

★One exercise I use to loosen up my seminar participants' thinking is to have them make up irreverent mottos for their products and organizations. Here are some of my favorite mottos; I won't reveal the company names because their lawyers don't always have a sense of humor. For a large international bank: **"Where you're not alone until you want a loan."** A large packaged-goods company: **"Where innovation is acceptable just as long as it's been tried before."** A very large computer company: **"Where creative people meet, and meet, and meet, and meet."** A large retailer: **"We put the 'cuss' in customer."** An airline: **"Customer service is our #1 priority — please leave your complaint at the beep."** A large consulting company: **"Not only are we smarter than you are, we're also younger than you are."** A large teachers' union: **"Lean to the left. Lean to the left. Stand up! Sit down! Strike, strike, strike!"** A software networking company: **"We're the glue that holds your problems together."**

"Sea water is both pure and polluted: for fish it's drinkable and life-giving; for humans undrinkable and destructive."

θάλασσα ὕδωρ καθαρώτατον καὶ μια-
ρώτατον, ἰχθύσι μὲν πότιμον καὶ σωτήρ-
ιον, ἀνθρώποις δὲ ἄποτον καὶ ὀλέθριον.

CHANGE CONTEXTS. If you say "Make me one with everything" to a teacher of religious mysticism, it signifies one thing, but to a hot-dog vendor it means something quite different. Similarly, if an amusement-park operator tells a middle-aged man, "I'll bring out the kid in you," one set of expectations will be created; but if an obstetrician says this to a woman in labor, a different result will occur. This is exactly Heraclitus' point in this epigram — life is filled with ambiguity and it is context that determines meaning.

Indeed, much of creativity is the ability to take something out of one context and put it in other contexts so that it takes on new meanings. The first person to look at an oyster and think "food" had this ability. So did the first person to look at a ship's sail and think "windmill." And so did the first person to look at sheep intestines and think "guitar strings," and the first person to look at a perfume vaporizer and think "gasoline carburetor," and the first person to look at bacterial mold and think "antibiotics," and the first person to look at baby's urea and think "skin-moisturizer ingredient," and the first person to look at a trapeze safety net and think "trampoline." And so do you if you've ever used a pen as a weapon, or a potato as a radio antenna, or flattened forks and spoons as the elements of a mobile, or a T-shirt as a tourniquet, or a telephone book as a booster seat. ❖ **In what different contexts can you imagine your idea? How does its meaning change?**

DISCOVER WHAT THRIVES. Just as polluted water can be life-giving for fish, even the most destructive situations may have positive effects. For example, for the second half of the twentieth century the Demilitarized Zone (DMZ) separating North and South Korea was probably the most dangerous place in the world. This ribbon of land — four kilometers wide and stretching more than two hundred kilometers through wetlands and rice paddies to rugged forested hills — was so heavily fortified and monitored by distrustful enemies on both sides that a careless error could conceivably have unleashed World War III. As a result of these heightened security measures, very little economic development has taken place in the DMZ or adjacent areas over the past five decades. This in turn has allowed the DMZ to become of one the world's great de facto wildlife reserves, inhabited by rare birds and animals including endangered cranes and egrets, bears, leopards, and tigers.

Similar examples of this phenomenon are the dying person whose terrible illness brings together estranged family members, or the tragic unsolved kidnapping that galvanizes a community, which bands together in sorrow and anger. ❖ **What's inhospitable in your current situation? Is there some way you could thrive despite the negative aspects of the situation?**

"On a circle, an end point can also be a beginning point."

ξυνὸν γὰρ ἀρχὴ καὶ πέρας
ἐπὶ κύκλου περιφερείας.

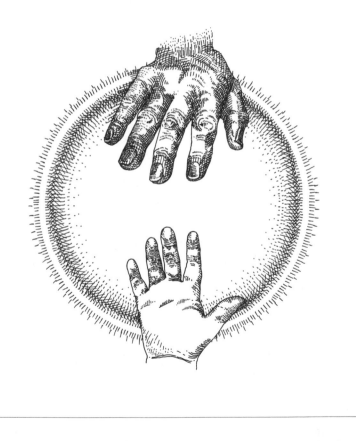

REFRAME THE SITUATION. Heraclitus understood that reality rarely presents itself to us with clearly defined boundaries. Rather, we impose our own order on the world through the concepts and categories of our language. If we change the words we use to describe a situation, we reframe it and change the way we think about it. For example: is the beach the end of the ocean or the beginning of land? Is a twelve-year-old female an old child or a young woman? Is the cocoon the end of the caterpillar or the beginning of the butterfly? Is water the end of ice or the beginning of vapor (or vice versa)? You could answer "Yes" to any of these questions. This shows that a thing, idea, or issue can be understood in a variety of different ways depending on how it is framed. ❖ **What other words and concepts can you use to describe your situation? What action did you take today that marks the end of one era and the beginning of a new era in your life?**

CHANGE VIEWPOINTS. If an end point can be a beginning point, can a kiss ever be an insult? It all depends on your point of view. Consider what happened when American soldiers dated English women during World War II. A problem arose: each sex accused the other of being sexually aggressive. Anthropologists say that every culture has a courtship procedure consisting of about thirty steps beginning with first eye contact on through to consummation. The interesting thing is that different cultures have different steps or put the same steps in a different order. In North America, anthropologists put kissing at step #5 — it's a friendly way of getting the relationship started. In pre-World War II England, however, kissing was about step #25 — it was considered a highly erotic activity.

Now imagine an American GI and an Englishwoman on their second date. The soldier thinks, "I'll give her a kiss to get this relationship going." He kisses her and she's astounded. She thinks, "This isn't supposed to happen until step #25." Furthermore, she feels as though she's been cheated out of twenty steps of the courtship process. But now she must make a decision: either break off the relationship because it's gone too far too fast, or get ready for intercourse because it's only five steps away. From the man's point of view, the situation is equally confusing: she seems incredibly formal and then reveals herself to be a nympho-maniac!

The moral: often we're not aware how much we're being guided by cultural assumptions. But if we look at our situation from the viewpoint of another culture, we just might see it in a fresh way. Remember also that we don't need to look far to find a "foreign" culture; we have only to look at what we ourselves are doing through the eyes of a teenager, a lawyer, a truck driver, a birder, a rock musician, or someone who must use a wheelchair, or even the point of view of someone from our parents' generation. Of course, a faraway culture — that of say Iceland or Borneo — is likely to challenge your viewpoint the most. ❖ **How would someone with a different set of cultural assumptions view your situation? What serious thing would they find amusing? What amusing thing might they take seriously?**

HEAR THE KNOCK OF OPPORTUNITY. A leading business school did a study which showed that its graduates succeeded initially, but after ten years were overtaken by a more streetwise group. The reason, according to the professor who ran the study: "We taught them how to solve problems, not recognize opportunities." What's the difference between these two activities? The problem-solver typically focuses on fixing what's broken, or making something whole again. The opportunity-seeker goes further, asking, "How can I take advantage of the ambiguity in this situation by trying something new? Where might that lead? What do I see that I wasn't paying attention to before?" In the same way that an end point can also be a beginning point, a problem can also be an opportunity for the creative thinker.*

Why don't more people approach life with this attitude? One reason is that many of us become "prisoners of familiarity." The more often we see or do something in the same way, the more difficult it is for us to think of doing it any other way.

---

*Poet T. S. Eliot, who studied Heraclitus, echoes him in this passage from the end of "Little Gidding" in the *Four Quartets*: "What we call the beginning is often the end/ And to make an end is to make a beginning./ The end is where we start from."

We get locked into looking back at what's familiar rather than forward into the different possibilities of what might open up. Inventor Alexander Graham Bell must have been thinking along these lines when he said, "When one door closes, another opens; but often we look so long upon the closed door that we do not see the one which has opened for us." ❖ **Think of a current problem. Rather than just fixing it, ask yourself: "What opportunities does it hold? How can I make it a beginning?"**

"It is disease that makes health pleasant, hunger that makes fullness good, and weariness that makes rest sweet."

*νοῦσος ὑγιείην ἐποίησεν ἡδὺ καί
ἀγαθόν, λιμὸς κόρον, κάματος ἀνάπαυσιν.*

EMBRACE THE NECESSITY OF OPPOSITES. One of Heraclitus' key insights is that opposites define and inform each other: it's very difficult to grasp the concept of "up" without "down," "hot" without "cold," "good" without "bad," or "beauty" without "ugliness." If one ceased to exist then the other wouldn't have much meaning. Each is the ground from which the other stands out. Furthermore, we don't fully appreciate something until we have thought about or experienced its opposite.

For example, success is more rewarding if we've tasted defeat, life more precious if we've been close to death, and love dearer if lost and regained. As German novelist Hermann Hesse, a student of Heraclitus, said in *Narcissus and Goldmund,* "Any life expands and flowers only through division and contradiction. What are reason and sobriety without the knowledge of intoxication? What is sensuality without death standing behind it? What is love without the eternal enmity of the sexes?" ❖ **What is the opposite of your goal? What must you do to avoid achieving it? Does thinking about the opposite of your goal make that goal clearer or more desirable to you?**

CONSIDER THE OPPOSITE VIEWPOINT. It's difficult to see the good ideas behind you by looking twice as hard at what's in front of you. Thus, reversing your viewpoint can be a good technique for opening up your thinking. For example, many centuries ago, a curious plague struck a small village in eastern Europe. Its victims fell into a deep coma, and most died within a day, though occasionally one would miraculously return to health. The villagers had a difficult time telling if a victim was dead or alive, but since most of the victims were dead, this wasn't a major problem. Then one day it was discovered that someone had been buried alive. An alarmed town council convened. The majority voted to put food and water in every coffin. This would be expensive but it would save lives. Another group proposed a cheaper solution: implant a stake in every coffin lid directly over the victim's heart. When the lid was closed, all doubts about the victim's condition would be laid to rest. What differentiated the solutions were the questions used to find them. Whereas the first group asked, "What if we bury somebody *alive*," the second group asked, "How can we make sure everyone we bury is *dead*?"

Suppose you're in charge of improving customer service at an airline. Focusing on how to *reduce complaints* will lead you to one set of ideas, while searching for ways to *increase customer letters of satisfaction to employees* will lead to a different set. Similarly, by reversing its focus from "cure" to "prevention," many doctors have moved the responsibility of health from the physician to the patient, and forced the latter to become more knowledgeable about the factors that constitute wellness. ❖ **How can you look at your situation in an opposite way? What do you see that wasn't apparent before?**

USE WHAT'S NOT THERE. One of the most significant but unheralded communications developments of the past 1,500 years is the adoption of spaces between words. Notice the words you're currently reading. They are separated by spaces, written in lower-case letters, and are fairly easy to read. Prior to approximately the eighth century C.E., however, Latin and Greek were written in capital letters in a "run on" fashion, that is, without spaces between the words. Here's an example: THEREARENOSPACES

BETWEENTHESEWORDSWHICHMAKESTHISA
LOTMOREDIFFICULTTOREAD. As you can see,
this type of writing slows you down. In ancient times,
though, Latin and Greek texts were almost always
read out loud. (This method is known as "reading
by ear.") Identifying words by sound instead of sight,
ancient readers had no difficulty with the run-on
written style. Literate Romans were sufficiently familiar with their own language that they didn't
need word-separating spaces to read aloud.

Eighth-century C.E. Saxon and Gothic priests,
however, had a weaker grasp of Latin, and so
couldn't always determine where one word ended
and the next began. The priests solved this problem by inserting spaces between the words to serve
as a recognition aid. Over time, the addition of
the spaces created an unexpected benefit: faster
reading. That's because if you can see the beginning and the ending of a word, you will recognize it
more quickly; the brain can "sight-read" words in
much less time than it takes to speak and hear them.
By the twelfth century, most of the literate world had
come to use spaces, and sight-reading became widespread.

When you look at a coffee cup, what do you notice? Its color? Its material? Its shape? How about focusing on the space within — that's what gives it its utility. When you look at the drawing that accompanies this Creative Insight (on page 127), what do you see? If you concentrate on the pen lines, you'll see a bird. But if you focus on the space, you'll see a question mark (and if you flip it upside down and then focus on the space, you'll see a seal balancing a ball on its nose). Along similar lines, piano virtuoso Artur Schnabel once explained the secret of his artistry by saying, "The notes I handle no better than many pianists. But the pauses between the notes — ah, that is where the art resides!" ❖ **Where can you create space in your situation? What benefits will that provide?**

ASK A FOOL. Carrying the strategy of "looking at the opposite side" to extremes brings us to the realm of the fool, the being for whom everyday ways of understanding and acting have little meaning. It's the fool's job to extol the trivial, trifle with the exalted, and parody the common perception of a situation. In the same way that "disease makes us appreciate health," the fool makes us conscious of the habits of thinking that we take for granted and rarely question.*

A good example is Till Eulenspiegel, the fourteenth-century German peasant trickster whose merry pranks were the source of numerous folk and literary tales. One day when Till was hiking in the mountains, he was seen to be crying while walking downhill and laughing merrily while climbing up. When asked the reason for his odd behavior, Till replied, "While going downhill I'm thinking of the

---

*Some people regard the fool as a simpleton, a dunce "whose elevator doesn't go all the way to the top," the imbecile "whose belt doesn't go through all the loops," the idiot "whose bell has no clapper," or the moron "who's a few french fries short of a 'Happy Meal.'" Nothing could be farther from the truth! A good fool needs to be part actor and part poet, part philosopher and part psychologist. The fool was consulted by Egyptian pharaohs and Babylonian kings. His opinion was sought by Roman emperors and Greek tyrants. He played an important part in the courts of the Chinese emperors. He advised the Indian chiefs of the Pueblo and Hopi nations. The fool was prominently employed by European royalty in the Middle Ages and the Renaissance. Because of his ability to open up people's thinking, the fool has been held in as much esteem as the the medicine man and the priest.

strenuous climb up ahead and that makes me sad; and, while hiking uphill I'm anticipating the pleasure of the easy descent."

The fool can also be irreverent. He'll pose riddles such as, "What does a rich man put in his pocket that the poor man throws away?" When he answers, "Snot," he forces you to re-examine the sanctity of your basic rituals. The fool can be cryptic. He'll say the best way to see something is with your ears. Initially, this may seem weird, but after you've thought about it, you might agree that listening to a story conjures up more images than watching television. The fool will take the contrary position in most conversations. Whereas many people would agree that, "If a thing is worth doing, it's worth doing well," the fool might say, "You don't have to do things well! Indeed, it's okay to do something poorly; otherwise you'll never let yourself be a beginner at a new activity."

In my seminars, I provide an opportunity for people to practice playing the fool. It's an exercise called the "Fools and the Rules." It's easy to play: you take your holiest "sacred cow" and sacrifice it on the altar of foolishness. In addition to being a lot of fun, this exercise is a great way to examine your assumptions. If you come up with no new ideas, at least you'll understand why the rule is there in the first place. Here are two of my all-time favorite examples.

Rule #1: "Always be polite on the telephone." Fool's Response: "Are you kidding? Abusive behavior cuts down on phone time. It also gives our public relations department more work. It would eliminate the hold button on the telephone as well as lead to honest employee relationships. Finally, rude telephone manners could serve as an outlet for employee stress."

Rule #2: "We are 'Committed to Excellence.'" Fool's Response: "How about 'Committed to Incompetence'? We'd have lower training costs, less development time, and less quality control. Also, part shortages wouldn't hold up production. We'd improve our chances of reaching our design goals. In addition, we wouldn't be afraid to try to new ideas; after all, what do we have to lose? Think of it from the customer's point of view: he would have a pleasant surprise whenever one of our products worked. He would have reduced expectations, and wouldn't be disappointed as often. In the past, we've been able to sell our products based on their technical merits. With mediocre products, however, we would have to learn how to sell. But then we would also have a larger market. There are more mediocre people in the world than excellent ones. We could even have a new motto: 'Nothing succeeds like mediocrity because everybody understands it so well.'"

The fool's job is to shake, assault, and massage the conventions that keep our thinking in a rut. He may not give us the right answer or solve our problems, but at the very least he'll give us a fresh appreciation of why we do things and perhaps jolt us into finding a better solution ourselves. ❖ **What would a fool say about your situation?**

"The doctor inflicts pain to cure suffering."

οἱ ἰατροὶ τέμνοντες καιόντες.

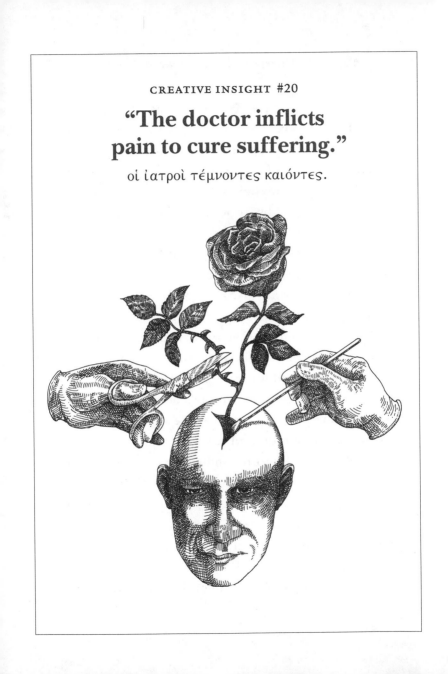

TURN LOGIC ON ITS HEAD. Heraclitus appreciated the paradox that sometimes the best way to reach an objective is to turn the most "logical" approach on its head. For example, the eighteenth-century British physician Edward Jenner discovered vaccination by inoculating healthy people with a dangerous but usually non-lethal disease, cowpox. This caused them to build up antibodies in their immune systems that prevented them from contracting a deadly disease, smallpox.

Here's another example: in 1334, the Duchess of Tyrol laid seige to Hochosterwitz Castle in Austria. As time wore on the defenders became desperate; their last food was an ox. The duchess's situation was also urgent: her troops had become unruly, and she had pressing matters elsewhere. Then the castle's commander had an idea that must have seemed utter folly to his men. He had the last ox slaughtered, stuffed it with grain, and threw it over the wall in front of the enemy camp. The duchess interpreted this to mean that the castle had so much food they could afford to waste it. By doing the opposite of what the duchess expected, the castle's commander convinced her that her siege wasn't working. Whereupon the discouraged duchess abandoned her siege and moved on.

To open up your thinking, try looking at what you're doing from an "unlogical" perspective. Suppose you're a teacher and ask, "What if I were less effective?" Perhaps the student would have to take more responsibility for her learning, which could lead to the development of a self-guided go-at-your-own-pace program. Suppose you're a basketball coach and ask, "How can I get my team out of sync?" The answer would be a list of unsettling things that the team could practice because they might have to deal with them in a game. Suppose you're a professional chef and ask, "What if I used less tasty food ingredients in my meals?" This could lead to ideas on how to improve the non-eating portions of the dining experience such as the food's presentation, the service, or the decor.

Doing the opposite of what's expected can also be an effective strategy in competitive situations such as sports, business, war, and romance. In most endeavors, we build up certain expectations about what the other side will or won't do. In football, for example, a third-and-long situation will typically cause the defense to prepare for a pass. In retail, you can bet that many stores will do a lot of "Back-to-School" advertising in late August. In politics, most candidates will have a last-minute media blitz. Sometimes doing the reverse of what people are expecting (a quarterback draw play, a "Back-to-School" sale at school year's end, media saturation six months before the election) can help you achieve your objective. ❖ **How might employing a reverse strategy enable you to reach your objective?**

ELIMINATE. If a part causes the whole to suffer, then remove it. For example, an editor reviewing a story might find a section that detracts from the whole and decide to cut it.* This may pain the author even though it's necessary to improve the overall work. ❖ **What needs to be removed in your situation? What pain will that cause? What relief will that bring?**

---

*This reminds me of the following publishing joke. Editor: "I like your story except for the ending." Author: "What's wrong with the ending?" Editor: "It should be closer to the beginning."

"The way up and the way down are one and the same."

όδὸς ἄνω κάτω μία καὶ ὡυτή.

RETHINK YOUR STRATEGY. In Heraclitus' world-view, things are continually changing. This means that every strategy that leads to the "way up" (success, progress, fulfillment) can ultimately become the wrong one and lead to the "way down" (failure, missed opportunity, stagnation). Thus, we need to be flexible with the strategies we use and change them when necessary. For example, what works for the caterpillar doesn't work for the butterfly. What's effective in parenting a two-year-old will be counterproductive when that child is a teenager. What a coach says to his players to motivate them in the preseason could backfire if said when preparing them for the playoffs. What brings results when a company is a start-up might be destructive when that same company is expanding into mature markets.

Cosmologist Lee Smolin relates that Albert Einstein was once asked why he didn't approach quantum theory with the same positivist philosophy that he had employed when he explored relativity theory. He answered that a good joke shouldn't be told too often. By this he didn't mean that positivism was a joke, but rather that any strategy that is fruitful in one stage of a scientific inquiry may be useless, or even lead to unreliable results, when applied at another stage. ❖ **Is the strategy that enabled you to get to where you are now the one you want to keep using? Conversely, is there an approach that you once rejected that might be appropriate in your current situation?**

WATCH OUT FOR "MORENESS." One strategy held dear by many is "more is better." For example, if you're a general fighting a battle, five divisions are preferable to three, or if you're a marketing manager building brand awareness, more television commercials are better than fewer. Sometimes, however, when things are made larger or their number increased they can take on a complex, new life of their own, and unexpected — even undesirable — things can happen.

For example, plants that grow tall to compete more aggressively for sunlight can become so heavy they fall over. Similarly, the purpose of hangars is to protect aircraft from the elements. But when their size is increased to shelter jumbo jets and dirigibles, they can create their own internal weather systems that rain on the vehicles being repaired. In like fashion, adding people to a project can cause it to function less smoothly.

This phenomenon is familar to those in project-management circles, and is probably best illustrated by the following story. The president of a large company went to his software department with the requirements for a new business application. He asked the manager, "How long will it take to design this system if five programmers are assigned to the task?" The manager, savvy in the mysteries of software development, replied, "One year." "But we need it now," the president said. "How long will it take if I tell you to assign ten programmers to it?" The manager frowned, "In that case, it will take two years." Clearly frustrated by this answer, the president asked, "What if I order one hundred programmers assigned to the project?" The manager sighed and said, "Then the project will never be completed." This wise manager knew that increasing the size of a project can create unexpected problems that were never apparent in the original smaller design.

Here's an example of how this works. Let's say

that you have a recipe for strawberry shortcake that serves four people. One day you invite over seven friends to eat this dessert. To make it, you simply double the recipe's proportions. On another occasion, you invite over one friend for this dessert. To make it, all you have to do is halve the proportions in the recipe. Now let's suppose that you invite fifty thousand people over for strawberry shortcake. At this point, the biggest challenges confronting you have nothing to do with the recipe. These include such things as buying strawberries on the commodities market, making deals with the Teamsters to deliver enough cream, traffic-flow coordination, and large-scale renting of chairs, tables, bowls, and spoons. The same things happen when projects become larger: issues come up that were not even thought about in the original plans. ❖ **Where would you be better served with less rather than more? What problems might "more" create?**

TRY THE REVERSE APPROACH. Heraclitus believed that unexpected things occur in the cosmos. Thus, if the "way down" and the "way up" are the same, then there must be times when the "way down" (or reverse strategy) can lead to the destination of the "way up." Indeed, if you've ever played hard-to-get to appear more attractive, gotten away from a problem in order to solve it, gone to the city to be alone, admitted helplessness to gain power, given away your possessions in order to feel rich, adopted a child's outlook to gain wisdom, or spoken very quietly to get people's attention, then you have used this counterintuitive strategy. ❖ **What counterintuitive tactic just might work in your current situation?**

Note: Because of its vivid similarity to Heraclitus' imagery in this epigram, I offer this classic creativity exercise put forward by novelist Arthur Koestler. "One morning, exactly at sunrise, a Buddhist monk began to climb a tall mountain. The narrow path, no more than a foot or two wide, spiraled around the mountain to a glittering temple at the summit. The monk ascended the path at varying rates of speed, stopping many times along the way to eat the dried fruit he carried with him. He reached the temple shortly before sunset.

"After several days of fasting and meditation he began his journey back along the same path, starting at sunrise and again walking at variable speeds with many pauses along the way. His average speed descending was, of course, greater than his average climbing speed.

"Your challenge: prove that there is a spot along the path that the monk will occupy at precisely the same time each day."

"A thing rests by changing."

μεταβάλλον ἀναπαύεται.

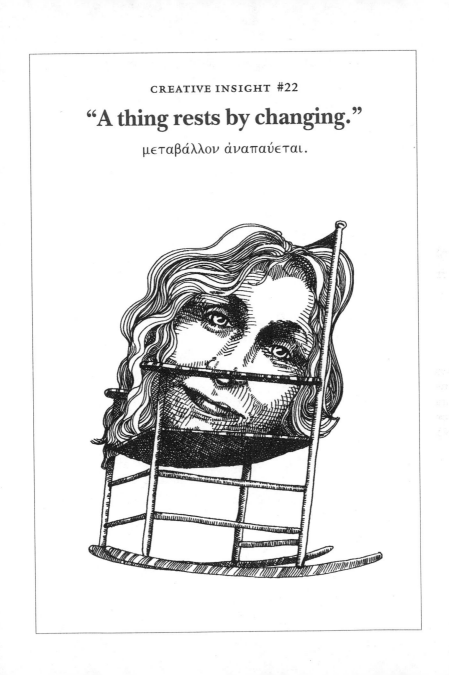

MOVE ON. This paradox poses the counterintuitive notion that change is more restful than staying still. It's resolved by understanding that Heraclitus believed that everything is continually changing, and that it often takes less energy to move on to the next phase of a process than to fight to stay in the current one. It's like rowing a boat on a river: it requires more effort to resist the current and remain stationary than to go with with the flow. Similarly, I find that if I allow myself to let go of a cherished position, strategy, or belief — especially one that takes increasingly more effort to hold on to — I'm more easily able to discover new alternatives. ❖ **Where would your energy be better focused — on where you've been or on where you're going? Is it time for you to move on to the next phase?**

BACK OFF. The flip side of this paradoxical epigram is that because things are continually changing, sometimes doing nothing — or at the very least, delaying action — can be the best course of action of all. This strategy of incubating a problem has several benefits for the creative mind. First, pausing for a bit allows you to put your situation in perspective. Over the years, I've asked many people when they get their ideas. Many say that it occurs when they are away from the problem altogether. They fill themselves with information about· the situation, and then get away from it for several days and let the good ideas percolate their way to the surface.

When you work at any task, you plant a seed in your mind. When you pause, the seed continues to grow in your unconscious mind. For example, if I asked you to name cities beginning with the letter "L," you would probably think of such places as London, Lisbon, Los Angeles, Louisville, and Las Vegas. But now that the task has been planted in your mind, you'll probably wake up tomorrow and think of five more "L" cities (Liverpool, Lima, Laramie, Lyon, and Leipzig) and continue to dig — at least unconsciously — for more after that (Leningrad, Laredo, Lhasa, Lucerne, and Little Rock).

Another benefit of delaying action is that while waiting you can gather more information about the most fruitful way to proceed on an issue. Designer Christopher Williams tells a story about an architect who built a cluster of large office buildings that were set on a central green. When construction was completed, the landscape crew asked him where he wanted the pathways between the buildings. "Not yet," the architect said. "Just plant the grass solidly between the buildings." This was done, and by late summer pedestrians had worn paths across the lawn, connecting building to building. The paths turned in easy curves rather than right angles, and were sized according to traffic flow. In the fall, the architect simply paved the pathways. Not only did the new pathways have a design beauty, they responded directly to user needs. Moral: pause for a bit and let the important things catch up with you. ❖ **What problems can you put off solving? What might you discover?**

FIND THE PARADOX. In the midst of a difficult problem, the Danish physicist Niels Bohr said, "How wonderful that we've met with a paradox. Now we have hope of making some progress." Bohr knew — as did Heraclitus, as shown by his fervent use of them — that paradoxes stimulate the creative process: they jolt our thinking and make us challenge our assumptions. In fact, it was

Bohr who proposed the seemingly paradoxical idea of complementarity, in which particles become waves and vice versa depending on how they are observed. Indeed, the act of "seeing the paradox" — the ability to entertain two contradictory ideas at the same time — lies at the heart of creative thinking.★

Each of the following paradoxical quotations forces us to let go of one viewpoint and embrace another. Confucius: "Real knowledge is knowing the extent of one's ignorance." Montaigne: "A man who fears suffering is already suffering from what he fears." Voltaire: "The superfluous is a very necessary thing." Pablo Picasso: "Art is a lie that makes us realize the truth." Eugene Ionesco: "Only the ephem-

---

★Heraclitus believed that creativity in the cosmos results from the working out and balancing of the opposing tensions that are present in all things. In another epigram, he says, **"Few appreciate how that which disagrees with itself is in agreement; the cosmos possesses harmony in contrariety, like that found in the bow and the lyre."** This idea resonates in the work of nineteenth-century German philosopher G.W.F. Hegel, and also in the thought of twentieth-century German philosopher Ernst Cassirer who used it as a cornerstone concept in his *Philosophy of Symbolic Forms.*

eral is of lasting value." Bertolt Brecht: "What happens to the hole when the cheese is gone?" George Wald: "A physicist is an atom's way of knowing about atoms." Thomas Hobbes: "Prophecy is many times the principal cause of the events foretold." Timothy Connor: "I have such a high regard for the truth that I use it sparingly."

Michel Foucault: "All modern thought is permeated by thinking the unthinkable." Martial: "The only wealth which you will keep forever is the wealth which you have given away." Seneca: "The hour which gives us life begins to take it away." St. Francis: "It is in giving that we receive, it is in pardoning that we are pardoned."

Goethe: "Where there is a great deal of light, the shadows are deeper." Barbara Ehrenreich: "We love television because television brings us a world in which television doesn't exist." Eden Phillpotts: "The people sensible enough to give good advice are usually sensible enough to give none." John Stuart Mill: "Ask yourself whether you are happy and you cease to be so." ❖ **What is paradoxical in your situation? How easily are you able to let go of one viewpoint in order to see a different one?**

CREATIVE INSIGHT #23

"The barley-wine drink falls apart unless it is stirred."

ὁ κυκεὼν διίσταται μὴ κινούμενος.

STIR THINGS UP. The *kukeon* or "barley-wine drink" was a sacred libation made by mixing together ground barley, grated cheese, and wine. If the drink were not kept in a state of constant agitation, the contents stratified and the *kukeon* as such ceased to exist. Our minds are like this.* If we settle into comfortable routines, our thinking becomes stagnant and rigid. (Indeed, I would argue that rigid thinking is not really thinking at all.) We need a challenge — such as solving a problem, pursuing an opportunity, having something at risk, or dealing with something new — to bring vitality to our minds.

This principle is illustrated in the following story. A frozen-fish processor had trouble selling a new line of fish because the fish tasted "flat." The

---

*For many years, I've believed that the human mind is like a big compost pile. It contains various ingredients — your knowledge and experience — all stewing together to produce something useful. For best results, you need to stir your compost pile periodically — the typical implement is a pitchfork — so that its components can breathe, mix, and properly ferment. Within this metaphor, you can think of Heraclitus as a "mental pitchfork," a tool with which to stir your mind.

company tried everything to keep the fish tasting fresh, including holding them in tanks until just before processing, but nothing worked. Then someone suggested, "Put a predator in there with them — that should keep them fresh." This idea solved the problem. The fish kept moving, retained their vitality, and tasted great. ❖ **What excites you about what you're currently doing? How can you challenge yourself?**

DETERMINE THE CONDITIONS FOR SUCCESS. Some things don't come into existence unless the right conditions are brought together: rainbows (when the sun is behind the observer, less than 42° above the horizon, and shining into rain), solar eclipses (when the sun, moon, and earth are aligned), political revolutions (when there is an economic downturn, vast social inequity, and an attractive ideology), procreation of mammals (potent, semen-delivering male and an ovulating, receptive female with a uterus capable of supporting growth), championship basketball teams (skill, coaching, training, teamwork, discipline, experience, fan support, and good fortune), and successful new product launches (exciting product, perceived need that is satisfied, good timing, reasonable price, targeted audience, effective marketing, and adequate supply to meet demand). ❖ **What are the conditions for success in your situation? If one of these is not satisfied, what will the result be?**

"While we're awake, we share one universe, but in sleep we each turn away to a world of our own."

τοῖς ἐγρηγορόσιν ἕνα καὶ κοινὸν κόσμον εἶναι, τῶν δὲ κοιμωμένων ἕκαστον εἰς ἴδιον ἀποστρέφεσθαι.

LISTEN TO YOUR DREAMS. Dreams contain symbols through which our unconscious mind speaks to us. We can use them to help us resolve conflicts, reach solutions, and find new approaches to obstacles in our lives.

How many times have you awakened from a dream and thought, "What was that all about? Why did I dream that I was catching bugs with my toothbrush? Why were Sappho and Bach sewing a quilt on my airplane? What did it mean that I was at the bottom of a valley and served a meal of rancid sandwiches and climbed halfway up only to find more of the same?"

At face value, dreams can appear to be weird or meaningless. But if you use them as a stimulants to your imagination, and try various ways of interpreting them, you may discover something that will lead your thinking in a new direction. For example, if you dream that someone kidnaps your children, you might take it as a sign that you should spend more time with them. It might also mean that you believe that someone is stealing your ideas. Or perhaps it means that you're being too serious and should be more playful.

Dreams have led to significant advances in science and technology. For example, chemist August Kekulé once dreamed of six circling snakes. This vision inspired his concept of the six-carbon benzene ring. He later said, "Let us learn to dream, then perhaps we will discover the truth." Elias Howe's dream of being attacked by spears with holes through their points led him to move the eye of his sewing-machine needle from its traditional position at the dull end to the point. Likewise, Russian chemist Dmitri Mendeleyev's periodic table was dream-inspired.

Dreams have played a crucial role in art, literature, music, and religion as well. The plot for *Dr. Jekyll and Mr. Hyde* came to Robert Louis Stevenson in a dream. As did the melody for "Yesterday" to Beatle Paul McCartney. Spanish artist Francisco Goya used his nightmares as the basis for many of his later works. Muhammad heard his prophetical call to found Islam in a dream. In one of the world's most famous dreams, the angel Gabriel came to Muhammad and guided him to Jerusalem on a silver mare and then to Heaven, where he received instructions from God.

I like to use the following technique to increase the likelihood that my dreams will enhance my creativity. Before going to sleep, I try to visualize a problem I'm working on. I don't try to solve it. I just try to picture it in my mind as clearly as I can. This plants the seed. Sometimes, I'll get an idea in the middle of the night, in which case I'll write it down — otherwise I'll forget it by morning. My best dream time is that "twilight zone" in the early morning when I'm coming out of deep sleep but I'm not yet fully awake. It's here that the mental categories that usually keep different ideas apart are softened, allowing different combinations of images to come together. It's these insights that I find to be particularly useful.

Your dreams are your own creations. Take advantage of the unique perspectives they provide. **❖ How can you relate a recent dream to a current problem? How did you feel in your dream? What parts of you do the different characters in your dreams represent?**

"Dogs bark at what they don't understand."

κύνες γὰρ καὶ βαύζουσιν
ὧν ἂν μὴ γινώσκωσι.

WATCH OUT FOR CRITICISM. New ideas are challenging by nature. They can threaten and disturb the existing order. Thus, most people have a warning device in their minds — a "barking dog" — to alert them to strange new ideas. Unless the new idea cleanly dovetails into what they are doing, people will often react to it by saying, "It won't work," "I don't get it," or "It's dumb," rather than "Gee, what a great idea!"

Many great innovations were at first greeted by barking dogs. For example, when the German astronomer Johannes Kepler correctly solved the problem of the planets' orbits by using ellipses rather than circles, he was met with great hostility. When the nineteenth-century Hungarian physician Ignaz Semmelweiss suggested to his fellow doctors that they could reduce disease by washing their hands in chlorinated lime water before inspecting their patients, he was denounced because his colleagues strongly resented the idea that they were "carrying death around on their hands." When composer Igor Stravinsky first presented his *Rite of Spring* ballet with its unusual harmonies and irregular rhythms, the audience rioted.

On the other hand, if the dogs are barking at your idea, there may be a good reason: perhaps your idea is unattractive, not well thought out, or badly presented. Your course of action should be to rethink your approach. Consider the barking to be a compliment: at least you're getting someone's attention. If an idea isn't threatening, it's easier to ignore it than to bark at it. ❖ **What negative reaction do you expect? How can you make your idea easier to understand and more attractive?**

MUZZLE YOUR OWN BARKING DOG. We tend to "bark" at other people's ideas — especially if they don't fit into familiar patterns. Of course, there are a lot of bad ideas and we need to avoid them. But if we are consistently overcritical, we may overlook strange but good ideas.

One thing I try to do when faced with an unusual or challenging idea is to avoid saying anything negative about it for sixty seconds. This allows me to create a context where I might see the idea in a positive light. During this period, I try to focus on its interesting and potentially useful features. If, at the end of a minute I still don't like the idea, then I can start barking at it.

An evaluation technique I employ when I work with another person is the "creative no." It works like this: either member of the partnership can veto the other's ideas. However, when this veto is exercised, the vetoer has to come up with another idea that both people like. Thus, this technique is both critical and constructive.

What are three benefits to wearing your clothes inside-out on Mondays?* How can collecting burned out light bulbs be a useful hobby?† ❖ **What in your current situation would benefit from a temporary cessation of criticism? What types of ideas do you bark at without ever really considering?**

---

*Clothes would last longer because they're worn on both sides. This also allows you to see where potential rips and tears are. You can display your sweat stains as "art." It might force you to have Monday as "work-at-home" day. It would make you buy clothes that were "soft on the outside" (e.g., no snaps or zippers) because you'd have to wear them next to your skin once a week.

†Here's one idea: cover them with papier-mâché, then break the glass to create rattles. Also, since they're generally viewed as worthless, they'd be inexpensive to acquire.

"Donkeys prefer garbage to gold."

ὄνους σύρματ᾽ ἂν ἑλέσθαι μᾶλλον ἢ χρυσόν.

PEOPLE VALUE DIFFERENT THINGS. What's important to one person can be of little consequence to another (how the Yankees perform in the World Series matters greatly to a New York baseball enthusiast but hardly at all to a Helsinki accountant). What's sacred to one group can be profane to another (a hamburger establishment on the corner of Michigan Avenue and Wacker Drive will attract customers; on the banks of the Ganges River it will draw outrage). What's unthinkable in one culture can be as natural as breathing in another (candy manufacturers in developed countries use special color agents to avoid staining the tongue; in developing countries, some people prefer having a candy-stained mouth because it boasts of having disposable income). Thus, your "golden idea" may be just garbage in someone else's estimation — and vice versa. As the eighteenth-century English literary figure Samuel Johnson put it, "So much are the modes of excellence settled by time and place that men may be boasting in one street of that which they would anxiously conceal in another." ❖ **Do other people value your issue the way you do? How can you help them understand your perspective? In**

what ways do you need to educate yourself about their point of view?

SIGNIFICANT WORKS REQUIRE EFFORT. If you're lazy, you probably won't achieve or create anything very important. In Heraclitus' view, most people are too easily satisfied with the "easy garbage" and are not willing to work for the more significant but "hard-to-get gold." Michelangelo had to endure seven years of lying on his back on a scaffold to paint the ceiling of the Sistine Chapel. Beethoven wrote four overtures for his opera *Fidelio* before he was satisfied. Soviet Union founder Vladimir Lenin spent thirty years preparing for his revolution. As World War II British Prime Minister Winston Churchill put it when asked to describe the most important lesson life had taught him, "Never give up, never give up, never give up." ❖ **What are you willing to sacrifice to reach your objective? How persistent are you?**

THINGS CHANGE THEIR VALUE. Sometimes the donkey isn't so stupid; at least its preference in this epigram — garbage — is generally edible. To say this in another way, be careful what you strive toward because it just might change its value. This moral is brought home in a provocative episode of the early 1960s television series *The Twilight Zone* entitled "The Rip Van Winkle Caper." Here's the plot: after robbing a bullion train from Fort Knox, four thieves stow their fortune in gold bricks in a cave and enter suspended animation for one hundred years, certain that they will evade all possible pursuit. When they awaken a century later, however, they find that their plan has worked perfectly except for one problem: when they try to spend their precious metal, they discover that it doesn't have the value they thought it would. Because of advances in industrial chemical engineering in the intervening years, gold has become a ubiquitous commodity and is actually worth less than its weight in water. It turns out that they are the asses! ❖ **Will what you're striving for still be valuable in the future? Under what circumstances might its value change? Might something you now consider worthless take on value in the future?**

CREATIVE INSIGHT #27

"Every walking animal is driven to its purpose with a whack."

πᾶν γὰρ ἑρπετὸν πληγῇ νέμεται.

EMBRACE FAILURE. Like other walking animals,* sometimes we need a good "whack on the side of the head" to get us focused on our purpose. One thing that "whacks" our thinking is failure — it jolts us out of our routines and forces us to look for fresh approaches. To a great extent, we function according to the principle of negative feedback. When things go smoothly, we don't think about them. Often it's only when things fail to do their job that they get our attention. We then realize that the current approach isn't working, and we need to come up with new and creative solutions.

For example, after the supertanker *Exxon Valdez* broke open off Alaska, polluting the coast with millions of gallons of oil, the petroleum industry was forced to rethink and toughen up many of its transport standards. After the explosion of the

---

*The ancient Greek word "herpeton" (ἑρπετὸν) in its later sense meant a four-footed animal. In its earlier Homeric sense, it was used by the gods when referring to humans. Heraclitus undoubtedly intended both meanings. Whether you're an ox, a horse, or a human being, you sometimes need a good "whack" to force you to pay attention to what's going on.

Challenger space shuttle, NASA changed many safety regulations. The sinking of the *Titanic* led to the creation of the International Ice Patrol and mandatory iceberg reporting.

Indeed, most people don't change when they "see the light"; they change when they "feel the heat." A friend of mine who had been fired from a job later told me, "It was traumatic at first but it turned out to be the best thing that ever happened to me. It compelled me to come to grips with my strengths and weaknesses as a person. It forced me to get out of my box and scramble." ❖ **How would failure affect what you're currently doing? What would you feel free to try?**

DISRUPT SUCCESS. Is success good? The answer isn't always obvious. Just as failure can lead to something good, sometimes success can lead to something bad. We can become complacent and think, "Everything is fine — since things are working, why change them?" As a result, we stop trying new approaches that may lead to something better.

Many times it's only when our success is threatened that we seek out improvements. A good example is the "sailing ship syndrome," named after the burst of innovation in the mid-nineteenth-century sailing-ship industry. Only after it became obvious that the steamship would sweep the commercial sailing ship from the seas did the sailing ship reach its peak of efficiency. Faced with the challenge of steam, sailing ships reduced the duration of the average westward crossing of the Atlantic from 35 days in 1839 to 24 days in 1860. Many of the changes that made this increase in speed possible could have been made decades earlier, but it was only when faced with elimination that the motivation was present to do so. Moral: to remain successful, sometimes we have to oppose or destroy the very things that enabled us to be successful in the first place. After all, every act of creation is first of all an act of destruction. ❖ **What previously successful assumptions can you challenge? What can you try that has a lesser chance of succeeding? When have threats led you to greater success?**

"There is a greater need to extinguish arrogance than a blazing fire."

ὕβριν χρὴ σβεννύναι μᾶλλον ἢ πυρκαϊήν.

YOU ARE NOT GOD. Self-confidence is essential to our success as creative human beings. That's because when we create new things, we expose ourselves to failure, frustration, ridicule, criticism, and rejection. Thus, it takes a strong sense of our own worth for us to persevere and make our idea a reality.

There is, however, a fine line between a healthy sense of one's abilities and arrogance. If you are repeatedly successful, there is a temptation to believe that you have found the "success formula" and are no longer subject to human fallibility. This is devastating to the creative process; in a world that is continually changing, every right idea or strategy eventually becomes the wrong one. With an arrogant attitude, you cease paying attention to differing points of view and information that contradicts your beliefs. You screen out the "boos" and amplify the "hurrahs." You believe that you're not subject to the same constraints as others.

For example, shortly before the Chernobyl nuclear reactor melted down and exploded, its engineering team (comprised of respected experts) won a distinguished award for operations productivity. The team felt that the safety rules they were asked to follow were designed much too narrowly for such an experienced group, and so they disregarded them during their reactor experiments. The result was a great catastrophe, with considerable loss of human life and potential genetic damage to untold future generations.

Think of all the businesses that were so sure of their products and methods that they stopped listening to their customers and soon found themselves without any. Similarly, the history of warfare is filled with military leaders who became intoxicated with their successes and then overreached in subsequent campaigns: Napoleon in Russia, Hitler in Russia, the French in Indochina, the Americans in Vietnam, the Soviets in Afghanistan. Arrogance can infect entire cultures. The Chinese were extremely confident of their superior ways shortly before they were conquered by the Mongols. The same could be said about the Aztecs and the Incas prior to the arrival of the Spanish.

The ancient Greek word for arrogance is "hubris," and it was seen as a precursor to one's downfall. Anyone proud enough to challenge the gods

will be burned by the gods. As surely as night follows day, destruction follows arrogance. ❖ **How is
your ego adversely affecting your judgment? Where
have you been successful in the past when dealing
with similar issues? Has this success made you less
receptive to alternative approaches?**

"Your character is your destiny."

ἦθος ἀνθρώπῳ δαίμων.

SET YOUR OWN COURSE. Life doesn't happen to us in a random, haphazard way. Rather, we determine our own destinies through the decisions we make. We decide what to pay attention to and what to ignore, what time to get up and when to go to bed, how hard to work and how much to play, how much to enjoy the moment, how much to save for tomorrow, what to share with others and what to keep private, when to persist and when to relent. I think of character as the "program" that determines what kinds of choices we will make in various situations.

Character consists of the parts of our basic nature that we let manifest themselves (and by corollary also those we suppress). It is shaped by our upbringing, education, culture, and experience. Do you tend toward being hard-working or lazy? Impetuous or cautious? Humorous or serious? Compassionate or tough-minded? By-the-book or likely to improvise? Aggressive or passive? Quick to come to closure or more likely to revisit a decision? Ready to seize on an opportunity or careful to study all the angles? Satisfied with "enough" or ever desirous of "more"? Selfish or altruistic? Get it done ahead of time or wait until the last minute? Introverted or extroverted? ❖ What parts of your character are likely to help you succeed in your current situation? What parts may cause you to fail? What will you have to suppress in order to be successful?

PROPHESY YOUR OWN SUCCESS. The worlds of thought and action overlap, as evidenced by the self-fulfilling prophecy. This is the phenomenon in which a person or group believes something to be true, acts on that belief, and thereby causes the belief to become a reality. For example, if consumers fear that there will be a shortage of a particular commodity, they may flock to the stores to stock up on the item, thereby disrupting distribution channels and causing an actual shortage. If a teacher believes that her students are gifted, she may go out of her way to cultivate their talents, inspiring the students to flourish in her classroom. If a team feels that it is jinxed against a particular rival, it will find a way to lose to that opponent. If investors think that market conditions will be healthy, they will invest their money, thus raising mar-

ket confidence and creating a healthy business climate. Similarly, what we think about ourselves has
a way of becoming true. If you think you're creative, you'll put yourself in situations where you
can use your creativity, try new approaches, take
risks, and come up with new ideas. If you don't
think of yourself as creative, you'll be too afraid of
your own ideas to give them a chance to work. Remember: as you think, so you are. ❖ **In what ways
can you see yourself succeeding? What self-fulfilling
prophecies — both positive and negative — are at
work in your life?**

CREATIVE INSIGHT #30

"The sun is new each day."

ὁ ἥλιος νέος ἐφ' ἡμέρῃ ἐστίν.

ANTICIPATE CHANGE. The cosmos is capable of surprising us. Problems spring up in places that were trouble-free only just yesterday. Opportunities suddenly emerge in long stagnant arenas. Routines that yielded predictable results stop working. A new person alters the group dynamic. Heraclitus reminds us that nothing is permanent and that we should not become slaves to our assumptions. Instead, we should attempt to keep our minds open about what is possible. ❖ **What's new in your situation? How has the cosmos surprised you recently?**

TAKE ANOTHER LOOK. Like the sun in Heraclitus' epigram, our own state of mind changes from day to day. For example, whereas on some days I'm euphoric over a recent success, on others I feel stressed and overwhelmed by problems. On some days I'm melancholic about the past, and on others I'm filled with hope about what's right around the corner. On some days I'm mentally exhausted and on others I'm alert and lucid. All of these different states of mind "color" the way I think about the problems, opportunities, and issues before me. ❖ **How is your thinking "colored" today? How does**

your situation appear with this perspective? Is the idea you reacted against yesterday really so bad? Does the idea you fell in love with last week still shine?

FORGIVE. If the sun is new today, perhaps other conditions have changed as well. If so, we might be able to let go of yesterday's disagreements. A benefit of this strategy is that it increases the number of creative options available to us.

For example, after World War I the victorious countries — still smarting from their huge financial outlays and vast number of battlefield casualties — demanded reparations from Germany. This imposition turned out to be the most costly political decision of the entire World War I era. Not only did it undermine Germany's economic recovery and weaken its already enfeebled political system, it also fostered the conditions that led to the rise of Hitler and the Nazis.

A generation later, after World War II, Europe again faced economic and political chaos. But instead of demanding reparations from the vanquished Axis powers, the Allies took the opposite approach in dealing with the situation. Through its massive Marshall Plan aid, the United States helped to rebuild much of the the continent's economic infrastructure, including Germany's. In doing so, it created conditions that encouraged both economic health and political stability. By not perpetuating past grievances, they broke the cycle of war and poverty that had cost the world tens of millions of lives in the first half of the twentieth century. ❖ **What can you forgive in your current situation? What new creative solutions does that open up for you?**

APPRECIATE THE "NOW." Since everything is changing, we should appreciate the "now" because soon it will be gone. All good things end. As the first-century B.C.E. Roman poet Horace put it, "*Carpe diem*": seize the day. If you find yourself in a bad situation, take heart: it too will pass. ❖ **What is good and beautiful in the present moment? What is unexpected?**

Final Thoughts

One of my favorite "Aha!'s" in studying Heraclitus came when I was writing the commentary for **"You can't step into the same river twice."** I realized that by stepping into the river, we change both the river and ourselves. This same logic applies to stepping into the Creative Insights: by meditating on these ideas on a regular basis, our own thinking is transformed and our creativity is enhanced.

Indeed, Heraclitus' enigmatic style in itself forces us to think differently. To understand his vivid metaphors and unusual paradoxes, we've had to tolerate ambiguity and probe for symbolic meanings. We've also had to be imaginative and think of multiple interpretations. These efforts, though, have been well-rewarded because we have discovered in his epigrams a treasure box of creative inspiration.

If we were to ask Heraclitus to reach into this treasure box and string several of his favorite jewels into a valedictory, I think his counsel to us would go something like this:

"The cosmos is continually changing. This is its defining characteristic. Thus, the world of today is not the same as yesterday's. This change creates both problems and opportunities for us.

"We're capable of recognizing patterns within this change. Go ahead and look for them. It is these patterns and our awareness of them that give life its richness. Some — like the solar halo that signifies the likelihood of rain in the next thirty-six hours — are readily apparent. Others — like the double helix structure of the DNA molecule — require ingenuity and effort to grasp.

"Find the good ideas right in front of you, but understand that these same ideas can prevent you from recognizing even better ones behind them. If an obstacle prevents you from moving forward, use it as an opportunity to try something different. Similarly, remember that knowledge is the stuff from which new ideas are made, but that forgetting what you know can also lead to surprising insights.

"Expect the unexpected, or you won't find it. You never know where your next idea will come from. Or where your just-conceived solution will lead you. Or what problems it might create.

"Reality is ambiguous. Just as the color blue represents 'mercy' in the Jewish Kabbalah, 'water' on physical geography maps, and 'carbon monoxide' on gas-canister labels, the situations we encounter can be interpreted in a variety of ways depending on the contexts in which we think about them. This ambiguity gives us the creative freedom to imagine alternative meanings.

"Studying the problem that is the opposite of the one you're facing will provide you with a fresh perspective. In addition, any strategy that leads to success can ultimately lead to failure or stagnation. Thus there are times when, in order to grow, you may have to let go of the very things that helped you attain success in the first place.

"Our own character counts for a lot. Curiosity,

playfulness, sobriety, and integrity are beneficial traits. Arrogance, laziness, and closed-mindedness are detrimental.

"Look for inspiration in many different areas, but above all look within yourself. Indeed, a sense of yourself is vital to your success as a creative human being. If, however, this sense of self-worth is carried to extremes, your judgment may become clouded and you risk cutting yourself off from the deep ocean of Being that sustains you.

"Finally, appreciate the 'now' but be willing to receive the next 'now' with a fresh set of assumptions. After all, each day presents us not only with new problems and surprises, but also with an opportunity to transform both ourselves and the rivers into which we step."

I hope you

enjoy and benefit from using

Heraclitus' wisdom to refresh

your creative spirit!

ANSWERS TO PUZZLES

Page 24: (1) Group 1 consists of letters that have vertical symmetry (left and right halves are mirror images of each other), and the entire set is: A, M, T, U, V, W, Y. Group 2 consists of letters that have horizontal symmetry: B, C, D, E, K. Group 3 is letters that have no symmetry: F, G, J, L, N, P, Q, R, S, Z. And group 4 is letters that have both vertical and horizontal symmetry: H, I, O, X. (2) All of the words contain three consecutive letters of the alphabet. A special bonus if you noticed that the word "stuffed" has three consecutive letters both forwards and backwards!

Pages 91-92: (1) The results of a beauty pageant had just been announced. The crying woman was the winner, and the "graciously" smiling women were the runners-up. (2) The woman is a fire fighter. While putting out a fire in the gallery, she sprayed water and fire-retardant foam on several of the paintings. This damaged them, but also prevented the destruction of the entire gallery. (3) Franz is a newborn baby, and a doctor is slapping his rear to get him to fill his lungs with air. (4) Irving spends his break sharpening his axe.

Page 109: (1) Freeze it. (2) One, because after that the barrel isn't empty. (3) Umbrellas. (4) A map.

Page 146: After trying a mathematical or logical approach, some people conclude that it would be a hghly unlikely coincidence for the monk to occupy the same place at the same time on two different occasions. But if you use a visual thinking strategy, you're on the "right path," as it were, to solving it. Imagine two monks starting simultaneously at sunrise, one ascending from the mountain base and the other descending from the summit. No matter what the walking and resting habits of each, there will be a point at which they cross on the path.

As a postscript to this exercise, on the morning I was writing this puzzle answer section I received the following correspondence from Allan Gillis in Toronto: "My friends and I were canoe tripping in Algonquin Park (a popular hiking and canoeing park in Ontario). We came to a long portage on a day when we were tired and hot. We had rented two canoes at the park outfitter, and they were heavy, but sturdy. We were sitting around lamenting the task ahead of us when another group came from the opposite direction — they were on their way back to the outfitter. They had also rented two canoes from the same outfitter. They were also feeling the heat and, rather than start with the canoes, they portaged their packs first and planned to return for the canoes. We chatted together, complaining about the task ahead of us carrying those heavy canoes through the woods over a rocky, hilly path of about two miles.

"Suddenly, I had an insight. I saw mentally the two groups meeting in the middle of the portage and it hit me. I proposed to the other group that we simply exchange canoes. They were all the same anyway and they were from the same outfitter. They agreed — we exchanged driver's license information in case there was any damage — and off we went. Both groups benefited from the exchange. All we had to do was carry our packs to the other side, get into their canoes and off we went! I never heard from the other group again, but I imagine that every now and then they think of that trip and the curious exchange."

About the Author

Roger von Oech created this book and also provided the translation. He is the founder and president of Creative Think, a Menlo Park, California company specializing in stimulating creativity and innovation. His seminars and presentations have enriched the creativity of many millions of people around the world.

He is the author of the best-selling creativity books *A Whack on the Side of the Head* and *A Kick in the Seat of the Pants,* and the popular *Creative Whack Pack* card deck.

He is a Phi Beta Kappa graduate of Ohio State University, and earned his Ph.D. from Stanford University in a self-conceived program in the "History of Ideas."

He is married, the father of two children, and resides in Atherton, California. He can be reached at:

Creative Think
Box 7354
Menlo Park, California 94026   USA

e-mail: rvo@creativethink.com
website: creativethink.com